# Access and Inclusion for Children with Autistic Spectrum Disorders

*by the same authors*

**Autism, Access and Inclusion on the Front Line**
**Confessions of an Autism Anorak**
*Matthew Hesmondhalgh*
*Foreword by Jacqui Jackson*
ISBN 1 84310 393 1

**The Autism Spectrum and Further Education**
**A Guide to Good Practice**
*Christine Breakey*
ISBN 1 84310 382 6

*of related interest*

**Specialist Support Approaches to Autism Spectrum Disorder**
**Students in Mainstream Settings**
*Sally Hewitt*
ISBN 1 84310 290 0

**Asperger Syndrome – What Teachers Need to Know**
*Matt Winter*
Written for Cloud 9 Children's Foundation
ISBN 1 84310 143 2

**Addressing the Challenging Behavior of Children with**
**High-Functioning Autism/Asperger Syndrome in the Classroom**
**A Guide for Teachers and Parents**
*Rebecca A. Moyes*
ISBN 1 84310 719 8

**Freaks, Geeks and Asperger Syndrome**
**A User Guide to Adolescence**
*Luke Jackson*
*Foreword by Tony Attwood*
ISBN 1 84310 098 3
Winner of the NASEN & TES Special Educational Needs Children's Book Award 2003

**Asperger's Syndrome**
**A Guide for Parents and Professionals**
*Tony Attwood*
*Foreword by Lorna Wing*
ISBN 1 85302 577 1

# Access and Inclusion
# for Children with Autistic
# Spectrum Disorders
### 'Let Me In'

*Matthew Hesmondhalgh*
*& Christine Breakey*

Jessica Kingsley Publishers
London and Philadelphia

First published in the United Kingdom in 2001
by Jessica Kingsley Publishers
116 Pentonville Road
London N1 9JB, UK
and
400 Market Street, Suite 400
Philadelphia, PA 19106, USA

*www.jkp.com*

**Library of Congress Cataloging in Publication Data**
Hesmondhalgh, Matthew, 1962–
   Access and inclusion for children with autistic spectrum disorders : let me in /
   Matthew Hesmondhalgh and Christine Breakey
      p. cm.
   Includes bibliographical references and index.
   ISBN 1-85302-986-6 (pb.)
   1. Autistic children--Education--Great Britain. 2. Inclusive education--Great
   Britain. I. Breakey, Christine, 1952– II.Title.
LC4719.G7 H47 2001
371.94--dc21

                                                                        2001037737

**British Library Cataloguing in Publication Data**
A CIP catalogue record for this book is available from the British Library

ISBN-13: 978 1 85302 986 8
ISBN-10: 1 85302 986 6

Front cover illustration by Sean Challis (a student at The Resource)

*For Kathryn,*
*who sadly could not come on the journey with us*

# CONTENTS

# Foreword

Looking back on my own childhood I knew something was different about me even before I received a diagnosis of Asperger's syndrome on 17 January 1989. I knew I was good at some things like using the computer, but not so good at other things like playing games. I was never picked for the school football team. I was fourteen and a half years old and at the time all the consultant psychiatrist could say about it (Asperger's syndrome) was that it is possibly a form of autism. Neither my mum nor I had ever heard of Asperger's syndrome before and all we could do was to look up the word 'autism' in the dictionary. This didn't particularly help, as autism was wrongly described as a psychiatric disorder. There was also little help from the National Autistic Society, as they themselves were becoming familiar with the term Asperger's syndrome. I can remember by chance watching a QED programme on television and being mesmerised by a young boy who was a similar age to myself and had similar difficulties. For example, at that time he could not tie his shoelaces but he had an amazing talent and could draw buildings from memory, to perfection. This boy was Stephen Wiltshire and he is autistic and is famous for his art.

Even after the diagnosis and after I received a Statement of Educational Need, it didn't mean anything then. No one translated the statement into giving me support. My worst time at school was feeling rejected and ignored and I felt like I was completely on my own. I didn't have anyone to listen to me and no one believed in me at all, or the diagnosis. Any improvement of my own situation at school was a direct result from the input of myself and my mum, who informed the teachers about autism and Asperger's syndrome. This information was very minimal, as there was very little about it at the time. There were no classroom assistants in the school and there was no one who was helping the teachers to try and understand me. Even the special needs co-ordinator didn't know about autism.

This book is about forming and developing equal partnerships between individuals with autism, their families and teachers. It is about two-way traffic: listening to the individuals and responding to their individual needs. The young people with autism being supported in mainstream education today should not have to go through what I went through. It is about developing and building upon their strengths and at the same time not forgetting areas in their lives where they will need support. This book is inspiring because it is based on real people who have complex needs and experiences. It shows how an organisation can develop into an 'autism friendly' service within a mainstream society which so often creates barriers to people with autism.

I wish this book had been written to help the teachers when I was at school. What I wanted was for someone to listen to me – as a whole person, not just looking at my autism. I wanted to be allowed to be me – and have someone believe in me. There are still people today who just see the 'impairment' and not the person. I would like people to see (a) the whole person; and (b) what they *can* do. There are examples of people with autism who have achieved great things, like Stephen Wiltshire and Temple Grandin. There is a distinct possibility that Mozart and Einstein both had strong autistic tendencies. It is okay to have autism and that is the message of this book. We need people like Matthew and Christine to help break down barriers so that more people with autism can achieve.

In conclusion, we need to remember that we can learn from people without autism, about autism. But the real experts are those people with autism. King Ecgbert School is an example of an organisation that not only believes in this principle, but has also developed the theory into practice. There are many skills and attributes that only people with autism can bring to this world, and we all have something to offer. The world would be a very different place without people with autism, and certainly not a better place. People with autism are unique, with their own individual personalities, and it is about us remembering this and developing an ongoing two-way traffic. Individuals don't need to be controlled. They don't need to feel fear or be afraid. They need the opportunity to be themselves and they need the people around them to give them support to make this happen. They don't need to be controlled; they need to be respected. Being autistic should not be an excuse to exclude people from mainstream education if that is what they need. Hopefully the readers of this book will be able to get it right for the many people with autism out there. Then we will really see what people can do.

Good luck.

*Richard Exley*

# Introduction

The Integrated Resource at King Ecgbert Secondary School in Sheffield opened in September 1994. We did not and still do not profess to have any answers. Staff and pupils have spent the last seven years trying to work out what the questions are. Our work is not complete. All of it is based on identifying a need and trying to remedy the situation. The needs are not just those of the child, but of other people who through no fault of their own have little knowledge or experience of autism. Our philosophy from the beginning was always to foster the attitude among all students of: 'I can achieve.'

It became the job of the staff team not only to teach, enable, support and guide our students, but also to engage other key people in a dialogue that would, it was hoped, give opportunities for this spirit of achievement to flourish.

The initial challenge was quite simple. Take a group of 20 pupils, all with a Statement of Special Needs relating primarily to a severe communication disorder, and integrate them into a pre-dominantly white, middle-class secondary school in the leafy suburbs of Sheffield. The school has excellent academic results at GCSE and a sixth form that was exclusive to A-level students.

Our students range in their academic ability from what could loosely be termed severe learning difficulties to genius level. The majority of our students have the label (or signpost) of autism. A smaller number have a diagnosis of Asperger's syndrome. A minority have severe speech and language disorders. The same size minority has Semantic Pragmatic disorder. We are not and have never claimed to be theorists. This is not a theoretical book. The boundaries between autism, higher level autism, Asperger's syndrome and Semantic Pragmatic disorder are not clear to us, while their similarities in a practical sense are. Psychologists, the medical profession and speech and language therapists deal with diagnosis, and our only hope is that the procedures, assessments and diagnostic tools improve quickly. To have an average age of eight for the diagnosis of Asperger's syndrome does not appear good enough to a lay person such as myself. Our most difficult cases are always those students who receive a late diagnosis. This is not just because of the sometimes horrific experiences which the child may have gone through in the education system, but also because of the pressure and anger caused within the family. Coming to terms with the fact that your child or teenager has a severe disability must take many years fully to accept.

This challenge led us on a journey that is not and never will be complete. Each new student we take teaches us things about autism that we have not confronted before. More questions are posed than answered. The disability itself is still in its infancy in terms of practice and experience. Only recently have we begun to hear the voices of people with autism. We have so much to learn from the adults of today who have coped with and managed their autism over the last 20 to 40 years. Their books, and the books of people with direct experience of the disability, have been brilliant tools of learning for staff in The Resource.

Unfortunately, we had few people to learn from when The Resource opened its doors seven years ago. The mistakes have been frequent, but nobody has been seriously hurt on the way. The students appear to be making good and in some cases re-markable progress. They remain our inspiration and our reason for continuing the search for more questions that challenge our non-autistic world.

This book is littered with stories. The Americanism 'action research' is much preferred to the word stories or analogies. This action research is something in which we should all be engaged, both parents and professionals, and so no apology is made for it. However, as with any kind of research, it is only useful if it prompts the next question and the next attempt, however inadequate and naive, at some possible solutions.

A brief word is needed about how and why The Resource was established. It was a remarkable piece of forward thinking by a man who has received little credit for his tireless work in the field. Rob Quayle was the head teacher of a primary special school for pupils with severe communication disorders in Sheffield. During the 1980s, he realised that there was a group of parents who felt that their children had made enough progress at his school (The Rowan) to warrant consideration for a place in mainstream education (with support) at the secondary stage. No such provision existed. Supported by a group of parents, Rob began to enter into a dialogue with Sheffield Local Education Authority (LEA) about rectifying this situation. As always in these situations, people of insight and drive are few and far between. However, Sheffield LEA was at that time blessed with a Principal Officer for Special Needs, Bob Chadwick, who realised the potential and opportunity to make a real difference for this group of pupils and their families. These two people began to put forward proposals and costings to Sheffield City Council. The cynic in me also realises that an increasing number of pupils with autism were being placed outside Sheffield for their secondary education because of this lack of suitable provision. The financial cost of this to Sheffield LEA was beginning to spiral. It took ten years to win the arguments and persuade a secondary school to let us in. To their credit, giving up was never an option. We could not let these two people down, let alone the parents who were depending on getting an integrated provision in a mainstream secondary school.

This struggle was backed all the way by parents and set the tone for how The Resource would be managed and developed. Rob Quayle now gives his experience and knowledge to our charity as an active trustee. Sadly, Bob Chadwick moved from Sheffield LEA to work in a nearby authority. He came to visit The Resource after we had been open for one year. The pleasure on his face and the respect he showed for our work was great to see. He has continued to follow the progress of The Resource. There was no way that I could forget the effort and determination of these two people. There was never an option of settling for second best. From the outset, The Resource was to be in the business of pushing back the boundaries a little further. This would never be a nine-to-five job; it would never be a five-day week job. This would be an extension of good parenting, which is, after all, a 24-hours-a-day, seven-days-a-week job.

In addition to picking up on the struggle of parents and these two professionals, The Resource appeared to be doing what the British national government wanted in terms of access and inclusion. We had already entered (albeit reluctantly on their part) into our first partnership, which was with the secondary school. This process of forging new and innovative partnerships was and still is being encouraged by the British government as good practice. However, the reader should note that the authors firmly believe in a range of provision for pupils with autistic spectrum disorders (ASD). The role of special schools is vital in this range of provision. Sheffield is blessed with some superb special schools in the primary and secondary sector that cater for pupils with autism and other severe communication disorders (SCD). The professional, dedicated and hard-working people in these schools do a first-class job. Integration and access in education must never be seen as a way of threatening special schools with closure or saving money. Since we began our work, one provision sadly lacking is support for pupils with autism and Asperger's syndrome in other mainstream schools. From the beginning, our telephone rang on a regular basis from mainstream schools who needed advice and training about autism and Asperger's syndrome. This is a group of pupils who receive inadequate levels of support and resources. Considering the research on how difficult the teenage years can be for someone with an ASD, this lack of support would seem shortsighted in terms of the financial cost to the LEA and social services departments if and when a crisis occurs.

Tony Attwood (Attwood 1998) uses the analogy of a brick wall to emphasise that every part of life for the person with autism has to be in place if progress is to occur. One 'brick' missing or out of line can jeopardise the whole structure of the wall. We have learnt that anxiety, stress and uncertainty can be missing bricks for our students. When discussing with his mother how he had settled into The Resource at King Ecgbert, Dominic commented that he felt like a lost piece of a puzzle that had found its jigsaw. This student's own 'jigsaw' is not yet complete and there are many pieces still missing, but at least he has found a safe place to work on it, with adults who can help to illuminate more of the picture. Given the right support, structure and encouragement, perhaps this same student will begin to enlarge this picture and add some inspirational bits of detail, shading and colour, which go to make up his individual personality.

# 1

# A Journey of a Thousand Miles
# Begins with One Step

We had one term to prepare a predominantly white, middle-class, high-achieving school for the arrival of our pupils. The parents of pupils in the school were not consulted. Pupils in the school were not consulted. Staff in the school received little or no information. There are so many things that I would do differently if we could start another integrated resource. The other new member of staff to the school was the head teacher. The previous head teacher had agreed to The Resource being sited in his school. It was one of his final decisions before retirement. It is fair to say that if the new head teacher had been given a choice about whether or not to have an integrated resource for pupils with autistic spectrum disorders (ASD) in his school, he would have answered in the negative. This is not a criticism of the head teacher of King Ecgbert School: over the seven years of working with him, Bob Evans has become one of our greatest supporters and a wonderful advocate for pupils with ASD and inclusion. I am sure he goes to conferences with other head teachers and sings our praises. He takes personal pride in what we have achieved. The local newspaper cuttings about our work take pride of place on his office wall. Our head teacher is somewhat of a computer expert, and this gives him something in common with one or two of our pupils. He has shown the same patience, understanding and interest in children with ASD that he does with all other pupils in his school. He celebrates the gritty, surprising D grades that some or our pupils achieve at GCSE with hard work and effort in the same way as he does the A grades.

The hostility about the establishment of The Resource at the school among some of my mainstream colleagues was understandable. It arose from a classic fear of the unknown. Most of our pupils would be coming from a small special school of 60 children. There they are taught in classes with no more than nine or ten other children. Some of them would not know how to answer their names at registration. The secondary school they would enter had over a thousand pupils on roll. The mainstream teachers had been led to believe that if pupils from The Resource were in their lessons, support would always be given. Perhaps one of the most frightening problems for me was that I had not set foot in a mainstream secondary school since being a pupil myself some fourteen years earlier. I had little idea about the format for GCSEs. I did not have the benefit of being able to do what the mainstream subject teachers did and they knew it. My A-level in history would be of little use in this new educational environment. The thought of going into a Year 7 French lesson began to fill me with the same kind of fear and boredom I remember feeling as a student myself.

Fortunately, Sheffield LEA took the very wise decision to do something technical sounding called frontloading the staffing ratio. In plain English this meant that they would allow the appointment of more staff in the early years so that a higher level of support could be offered to the overworked mainstream teachers. Our pupils would be given every conceivable advantage in order to have access to this strange establishment called a comprehensive secondary school. The first appointment made to the team was an excellent support worker with an extensive background in mainstream education. She became my guide in those early few weeks.

In that first term without any pupils, the school very kindly cleared out the drama storeroom so that I had what could loosely be termed an office. This was well out of the way of the hustle and bustle that goes on in schools, so I spent my first few days with a secure and quiet hiding place. I allowed myself brief and hurried excursions out of this tiny room, but never strayed too far in case I needed to beat a hasty retreat. Unfortunately, the toilets were right at the other end of the building, which was a real nightmare. My office was also near the area that would see extensive building work creating The Resource base. Suffice it to say that I did not see any sign of builders' bottoms, or those of electricians and plasterers for several months. I quickly had to investigate the intricate network of people responsible for designing, planning and actually carrying out the building work. In the nicest possible way, I became a thorn in their side.

After several days in hiding, I made a point of inviting myself into the lessons of every teacher in the school. Looking back, this request took so many of the teachers by surprise that they had little option or time to refuse. I took notes on things such as how much sarcasm was used, how long they stood at the front and talked, their style of humour and their methods of discipline. One thing that struck me, having worked only in special schools, was just how wonderful the mainstream pupils were at communicating. Sometimes they would ask me questions, naive enough to believe I might be able to help them. One 11-year-old girl in an English lesson put up her hand, so I proudly strolled over to give her the benefit of my vast experience. She pointed to a sentence in her book that included the term 'sexual deviance' and asked me in a loud voice just what was meant by this. Red-faced, I quietly suggested she should ask the proper teacher. We still smile if we pass each other in school and she is now an A-level English student.

The formal, traditional teachers posed no difficulties. They insisted on firm classroom rules as far as behaviour was concerned. Their lessons were quiet. Excellent instructions were given at the start with supportive guidelines written on the board or on a worksheet. They differentiated work by knowing their pupils well. The bright, able pupils were expected to reach set targets which appeared incredibly high to me, while the children of a lower ability had to work equally hard to achieve their set goals. Expectations about work and behaviour were high, and the overwhelming majority of pupils strove to live up to them. The explanations given about homework were clear and concise with time for questions. What was handed in was always praised, assuming it was the pupil's best effort. Group work was not often attempted. I was astounded at the professionalism and dedication of these teachers. The amount of work they must be putting in at home with preparation and marking left me feeling totally inadequate. Their knowledge in terms of the specific subject and curriculum, coupled with their obvious love of teaching children, was inspirational. The quality of work produced by all pupils was superb. When they attempted something slightly different, it was only to raise questions in those already inquiring minds. These teachers had no hesitation when it came to including me as a teaching resource. In a history lesson I found myself arguing from the point of view of an IRA freedom fighter, while the teacher took the opposing Protestant standpoint that one person's freedom fighter was another person's terrorist. The pupils in that lesson quickly got the idea that history depends to some extent on a person's point of view. I must have argued well because some of the pupils in that lesson still remind me about it several years later. The pupils coming to The Resource would fit well into these types of lesson.

A small number of lessons worried me. English was one subject that I began to think might cause problems. This was not because the teaching was poor, but rather because of the use of drama. This was great for mainstream pupils. However, these more open-ended lessons were based on ideas, abstract concepts and lots of group work. The dividing lines between reality and fiction might be difficult for some children with an ASD. Physical education (PE) gave me some concerns mainly because of the acoustics of the two gymnasiums. With the difficulties that some of our pupils might experience in screening out unwanted sound, their listening skills would have to be at a premium. It had nothing to do with the fact that I did not want to support rugby lessons in the middle of winter on a pitch that resembled a mud bath. Technologies such as the old-fashioned wood and metal work would be a whole new experience for our pupils. The noise of machinery and movement of pupils in these lessons scared me, let alone 11-year-old pupils with an ASD who would be coming from a small, quiet special school. Food technology (home economics or cookery to the uninitiated) just left me feeling bewildered. Pupils still cooked, but the lessons seemed to be about production techniques, packaging and follow-up surveys. The brevity of the period of time allowed for instruction before these secondary aged children were expected to 'get on with it' and use their own initiative and ideas was quite staggering. I was still stuck in the era when most teachers just gave you dictation and expected you to learn 'the word'.

To complicate matters further, disagreements occurred about how we should best integrate pupils into this mainstream environment. Should pupils work from The Resource base or be 'thrown in at the deep end'? It was assumed that the pupils' prior knowledge and understanding of mainstream education ranged from limited to non-existent. Yet we did not truly know how they would respond in the mainstream lessons. It certainly would have been a safer option to work from The Resource base and integrate gradually into areas where we could almost guarantee success. Believe me, there were days when 'safe seemed right'. However, it was felt that by doing this our pupils might miss out on opportunities where they could succeed. We could not deny pupils the opportunity to integrate. This meant taking a risk. The risk was taken, the challenge accepted. Our pupils would try all mainstream lessons (except religious education, RE). RE worried me the most because it seemed almost totally based on abstract concepts. In addition to this, I found that the RE staff had to work hardest at maintaining discipline in their lessons. RE lessons have undeniably come a long way since I was at secondary school, but they still had some way to go when we descended on the school. Staff in the department have changed several times since then (apparently RE teachers are just as hard to find as those who teach maths) and the improvements have been noted. Perhaps our pupils will be going into RE lessons by the time you read this book.

This approach gave the new pupils 24 hours a week in mainstream lessons and only one withdrawal hour. This one hour a week in The Resource was never going to be quite enough. The amount of pressure and stress we would be placing our pupils under by integrating for 24 hours a week could not be underestimated. In addition to the educational curriculum, pupils with ASD have a second curriculum (the social one) to learn. As Tony Attwood (2000) points out in a paper on homework: 'throughout the school day they rarely have an opportunity to relax'. There were no books to which we could turn for guidance on how much relaxation time a pupil with an ASD needed. Were we expecting too much? However, in *Autism: Preparing for Adulthood*, Patricia Howlin asserts:

> For the majority of high functioning children with autism, their chances of living a full and independent life will be dependent on whether they are able to obtain academic qualifications at school, which will, in turn, allow them to progress to further education and eventually a job. With few exceptions, the only way in which this can be achieved will be by attending a mainstream school. (Howlin 1997, p.143)

How would our pupils respond in the French lesson, the noisy technology room, and the cold and wet playing fields of Sheffield? Could they sit in an assembly with 200 other pupils? Some of the simple rules that dominate secondary education began to impress me. As a pupil myself these same rules and rigid timetable had depressed and suppressed my feelings of being an individual. However, for pupils with an ASD, I could see the fixed start and stop times working in our favour. Bells ringing to warn pupils of the impending doom of the next lesson would be very clear non-verbal signs to our pupils that it was time to move. Homework diaries were used to record how much needed to be done and when it was due in to the teacher. The simple rule of calling a male teacher 'Sir' and a female one 'Miss' appeared to be quite straightforward. Registers are always called in the same order. If a pupil wanted to eat cheese flan, smoky bacon flavoured crisps and strawberry jelly for lunch five days a week, it was possible.

It became vital to write a mission statement about our aims and philosophy. This began a search that wasted a great deal of time and is a mistake which we still make to this day. Naively, I felt that there should be some wonderful fountain of knowledge to which we could turn for guidance and inspiration. After all, there was little point in 'reinventing the wheel'. I had visited some superb units in Oxfordshire (The Chinnor Resources). They were not quite what I had in mind for Sheffield, although I did learn a lot from this visit. However, nothing I could find was quite right. It became clear that if we wanted to do things our way, then a mission statement would have to be written the way we wanted it. This theme is one that has been underlined several times over the last six years. There are no short cuts. Our mission statement is shown in Figure 1.1.

---

### Mission Statement

The Integrated Resource at King Ecgbert School aims to promote the development of pupils with severe communication disorders both as individuals and communicators, by providing a high quality special educational service within a mainstream secondary school.

These disorders may either be specific or complex in nature, but will generally be long-term.

## General aims

In order to achieve this aim, The Resource will endeavour to:

- Provide equality of opportunity and access to a broad, balanced and differentiated curriculum that is relevant to the rights and entitlements of our pupils, as well as their special educational needs.
- Provide a multi-professional approach to assessment, teaching, therapy and vocational guidance of the pupils, which is located within a framework of the school, but is additional to it.
- Enable and support all pupils to gain as much social contact, experience and shared learning with their peers as is in their best interests and those of their peers.
- Promote a partnership with parents that is collaborative, informative and supportive.
- Provide an environment which is safe and secure, meets their physical and emotional needs, and has sufficient resources of an appropriate type.

## Admission criteria

The Integrated Resource provides special education for pupils who have been formally assessed and have a Statement of Special Educational Need that relates to a severe communication difficulty or disorder. This difficulty may either be:

- a specific speech and language disorder, i.e. a pattern of speech and/or language development that significantly deviates from that expected, and does not arise out of learning English as a second language, relate to a general developmental delay, or a primary sensory, physical or emotional difficulty
- or a complex communication disorder, including autism and autistic spectrum disorders, that

involve qualitative impairments in the development of reciprocal social interaction, verbal and non-verbal communication, imaginative activity and may also show in restricted patterns of behaviour, interests and/or activities.

The pupils placed in The Resource will be those who, given appropriate support, can:

- cope with and benefit from access to a mainstream curriculum
- cope with and benefit from access to a mainstream environment and peers
- cope with and benefit from progressively increasing amounts of independence.

## General considerations

Severe communication difficulties, including autism, can coexist with varying degrees of learning difficulty. The general levels of achievement/performance are not only a function of the degree of communication difficulty experienced, but also a function of the degree of learning difficulty. The communication difficulty determines the approach required, and the learning difficulty determines the type/level of curriculum followed.

## Specific advice

In order to place a pupil appropriately within a range of provisions, it is necessary to obtain professional opinion regarding the potential for developing full/partial independence in learning and living. At secondary transfer, this should be available from consideration of the past six years' rate of progression.

Communication therapy and advice will be an essential requirement for all pupils within The Resource, as the communication abilities will determine (along with the learning abilities) the degree to which a pupil will be able to take advantage of a mainstream curriculum. The behavioural skills and difficulties of a pupil will determine the support and supervision needs, which may affect placement decision.

Social interaction may be difficult for some pupils and account needs to be taken of this, especially the vulnerability of an individual pupil to peer pressures such as bullying, manipulation and exploitation.

## Philosophy

The philosophy of The Resource stems from the belief that all children are able to learn and make progress. The Resource will promote access to the curriculum for pupils with severe communication disorders by:

- providing teaching support within the classroom
- providing access to individual and small group teaching where appropriate
- providing access to resources
- providing information on the additional needs of pupils in The Resource
- promoting a programme of in-service training for staff in The Resource and the school as a whole.

## Principles

The principles that guide this philosophy are as follows:

- All pupils with special or additional needs are entitled to access the full curriculum, including the National Curriculum.
- Pupils with additional needs should be educated in mainstream classes wherever possible.
- Support must be provided, as appropriate, to ensure that any communication and learning difficulties do not become an impediment to educational and social progress.
- The needs of pupils and staff should be reviewed on a regular basis.

## The Environment

The environment of The Resource will be based on the following ideas:

1. The Resource will be pupil-centred, starting from where the pupil is at and encouraging him/her to be an active participant in his or her learning.

2. Importance will be placed on developing predictable daily routines with clear expectations.

3. Support and guidance to alleviate fears, anxieties and misunderstandings will be provided.

4. Pupils will be encouraged both as individuals and as members of a group to have times of genuine control and responsibility for their environment.

5. Adults will be encouraged to accept pupils' attempts to initiate conversation, with them being responsive to the pupils' meaning and intention.

6. Adults will be encouraged to be aware of the pupils' needs for self-esteem. Pupils will be encouraged to develop perceptions of their own strengths, as well as weaknesses.

7. Emphasis will be placed on independence in learning skills and problem solving. The aim is to build expectations of: '**I can achieve**.'

## Conclusion

The Resource does not have all the answers. Staff, pupils and parents are involved in a learning process. We need time and co-operation to allow us to get on with the job in hand.

*Figure 1.1 Mission Statement*

This mission statement may not suit your needs if you are in a similar position. There may be parts you like. Save yourself some time, write all documents to suit your dream, your ideal and the needs of the children with whom you work.

The two pupils we would start with as Year 7s began to prepare for their transfer to King Ecgberts. This preparation had to be thorough, reassuring to both pupils and their parents, and able to give staff some idea about their relative strengths and weaknesses. It is something I feel we do very well and got right from the start. During their final term in the primary special school, the two pupils for transfer visited King Ecgbert's on six occasions. The first visit was for just half an hour. I stood with these two pupils and we watched several hundred pupils file past us as they moved to their next lesson. It was noisy and scary. The two pupils sat in on some lessons. Using maps we found our way around both the school buildings. They had their dinner at the school. The preparation was good and they could not wait to start at the school. The only area they could not see was The Resource base. I began shouting at someone dressed in overalls, only to realise it was the caretaker.

A written outline of the pupils' additional needs was produced by taking advice from parents, previous primary teachers and speech and language therapists. This became something we could give to mainstream subject teachers – something to read from day one. One of these outlines is shown in Figure 1.2. This outline would dictate our approach from day one of a pupil starting with us. We had to attempt to start from 'where the pupil is at'.

Some mainstream teachers would inevitably lose this outline of additional needs as they were deluged with paperwork in the first few weeks of a new academic year. I am not sure many people outside education realise how many different roles the teachers in schools have to play. In addition to the task of teaching, they are accountants, administrative workers, cleaners, social workers and therapists. A follow-up copy of the outline of additional needs

# Outline of additional needs

## Joe Pretend. Form: 7XX

## Additional needs

Joe comes to us from The Willows School. He has social and communication difficulties associated with autism. Joe processes language slowly and will need extra time to formulate expressive language. He can also have word-finding difficulties. Joe may be literal in his interpretation of language. He will require extra 1:1 instructions and must be permitted to ask for clarification. He will need clear explanations about classroom rules, and then may become upset if others break them. He can respond badly to direction or even gentle criticism. He can become upset and opt out if he considers the work too hard. Joe is still unaware of everyday danger, e.g. traffic. Nobody has ever said being autistic is easy. However, do not despair, because Joe has many strengths.

### Areas of strength

1. Joe will listen to explanations and can be reasoned with.
2. He is described as having good basic numeracy and literacy skills.
3. Joe is kind, well-mannered, always co-operative, and will respond well to responsibility.
4. Joe is developing a sense of humour (*usually a tricky area for someone with autism*).
5. Joe is sociable and enjoys talking to adults and peers.
6. He has good visual skills and memory.
7. Joe uses reference books and dictionaries with confidence.

## Areas of greatest difficulty

1. Social interaction – Joe can be opinionated and unaware of the feelings of others.
2. Joe can be over-sensitive to criticism.
3. Joe can appear rigid in his attitudes and approaches.
4. Joe does not like to fail.
5. Joe's organisational skills are poor. He will lose books/coats/rulers, etc.

## Suggestions

1. Joe will need clear and concise instructions.
2. Joe must be forewarned about any changes to his timetable, rooms or teachers.
3. Joe needs encouragement to try new things and to know he may get things wrong the first few times.
4. Joe will get opportunities to talk through any difficulties with a member of staff from The Resource.
5. He will need additional time to process verbal information and his responses to it.
6. Visual material will greatly aid his learning.
7. Joe will have a 'glossary book' to write down new vocabulary and meanings.

**If you have any suggestions about Joe, or experience any difficulties with him, please do not hesitate to talk to a member of staff from The Resource.**

Joe is not a pupil we know well. We will be learning about his strengths and difficulties at the same time as you. We will need to develop and improve our approaches towards Joe. Your patience and understanding in the first few terms will be much appreciated. Some of the rigidities/behaviours presented at the primary stage do reduce in severity at secondary school, mainly because of the structure of the timetable.

**Copies to:** All mainstream subject teachers of Joe Pretend.

*Figure 1.2 Outline of additional needs*

was usually worthwhile. The information would also be useful for teachers on supply and student teachers within the school.

One particular influential member of mainstream staff appeared to need to develop her understanding of autism more than most. It was felt that she was causing some unrest among a section of staff at the school. She happened to be a member of senior staff and the head of sixth form. Mrs Smith was a lovely person, but no mission statement or outline of additional needs was going to cause a rethink of her position. Our pupils would need to be her teachers and a strategy had to be developed: for strategy, read 'trick'. Our two pupils who began their Y7 at King Ecgbert School were under immense pressure from the start. We were making up a strategy as we went along and they were 'our firsts'. However, it was decided that whenever these two pupils passed Mrs Smith on the corridors of the school, they would greet her with the appropriate 'Good morning' or 'Good after-noon'. They were also encouraged to enquire about the health of Mrs Smith once a day on the first meeting. One of these pupils did this religiously and without question. Over a number of weeks, it was our pupils who had the most influence over Mrs Smith.

An introductory teaching package was written for use in the first year. This had to include lessons on road safety as King Ecgbert's has the misfortune to be a split site school with a busy road in between buildings. From this point of view, we could not have landed in a worse school. Most of the pupils we take have little or no experience of crossing a road safely. It is the pupils who change buildings at King Ecgbert school rather than the teachers. This means that at 'change-over time' (the gap between one lesson finishing and the next one starting) there could be as many as 500 mainstream pupils on the move between buildings. Most of these cross the road at roughly the same time. The potential for disaster is huge and teenagers (especially boys) are in the highest risk group in terms of road accidents. While staff would be crossing the road with pupils, we did feel it was important to aim for some degree of independence in this, which could only be done with agreement from parents. Some of the lessons on road safety are shown in Figure 1.3. Again, these programmes were written by staff to suit the needs of the pupils and the situation in which we found ourselves.

---

### Lesson 1

#### Aim
To establish that the pupil properly understands the vocabulary used in road safety.

VOCABULARY LIST TO TEACH/CHECK

1. Pavement
2. Road
3. Kerb
4. Traffic
5. Speed
6. Distance
7. Signal/indicate
8. Risk/chance

#### Resources
Picture sheets and test sheet.

#### Tasks
1. Discuss the pictures using the agreed vocabulary.
2. Go out of school and observe the road and road users. Experience these words.
3. Support the pupil by filling in the test sheet for this lesson.

### Lesson 2

#### Aim
To understand the signals given by drivers to indicate what a car is going to do.

#### Resources
Pens/paper. Two worksheets.

---

---

**Tasks**

1. Go out with the pupil(s) near the road between the two school buildings.

2. Observe 20 vehicles as they turn left/right out of the road.

3. Fill in the table to show whether a driver indicated or not.

4. Return to class and discuss the results. Do most drivers indicate or not?

5. Conclude that while it is very important to watch for the signals of drivers because of the clues they can give us, we still need to **wait, watch** and see what a driver **actually** does before we finally decide if it safe to cross.

6. Encourage the pupil to attempt the question sheet.

---

*Figure 1.3 Road safety lessons*

There are three more lessons in this work on road safety. Risk taking is a huge area of teaching and never an easy one. I particularly like the lesson that examines concentration and focus. The pupils are given a sheet with numbers from 1 to 30 in random order. They are timed as they touch the numbers in order. This is easy. The same exercise is repeated but the pupil has to recite a well-known nursery rhyme or sing a favourite pop song. The exercise takes much longer because the focus is split between the two activities. Relating this to the act of concentrating when a pupil gets to the point of crossing a road still takes some work. But the lesson is great fun.

The Introductory Teaching Pack has lessons on finding your way around the two school buildings, learning the names of teachers and their departments (by using photos and name cards), answering your name on a register, listening skills and copying information from a board accurately and quickly. None of these are as important as the road safety lessons. What makes road safety easier for our pupils is that, in addition to the lessons, they are crossing the road with support on a daily basis. However, no pupil is allowed to cross the road at the end of the school day. This is because there are three schools in the area and the road is extremely busy at the end of the school day. Risks can be taken so far, and then they become avoidable danger.

Furniture had to be bought for The Resource base and Sheffield LEA gave me £1000. There was no building in which to put furniture, but that was a minor difficulty. The building work to the area of school that would become our base was a nightmare. From my spyhole in the drama cupboard I would wring my hands in despair each time I failed to see the arrival of anyone who even loosely resembled a builder. The advantage was that I could tell the architect what I wanted. On paper, The Resource was going to be designed using my ideas from the start, and we were blessed with a brilliant architect. She listened patiently to my ramblings about not wanting any perpendicular lines, designing cupboard space that would not be too intrusive, where to position sinks and, most important of all, the colour scheme. I picked a beautiful terracotta colour for the walls, which in reality turned out to be orange. In addition to two small classrooms and a computer room, I wanted to create a 'living space' to promote relaxation and communication, a bit like the living room of a house perhaps. This would have easy chairs rather than classroom ones and carpets rather than tiled flooring, with lots of natural light – different from the usual special needs departments found in most secondary schools. This would be a place to sit, drink coffee, chat and laugh. It would become the heart of The Resource for pupils and staff alike, a home from home. I also wanted to encourage mainstream pupils to use The Resource at dinner times. This would be inclusion in reverse if you like.

Communication between school and home appeared to be a major difficulty. It was felt that parents would need daily reassurance that their child had done well. They would need information, however brief, about what had happened that day. This could then be used to initiate conversations at home, as well as keeping parents up to date with events. We would need good information from home on a daily basis. If it had been a tough night at home, we would need to know about it immediately, so we could act accordingly. We hoped to have a high degree of consistency between approaches used at home and school. Homework sometimes needed to be explained in greater detail. Reminders had to be given about bringing PE kit or ingredients for a food lesson. Important letters from school could remain in the bottom of a school bag for weeks if the pupil forgot about it (this is not a problem unique to children with severe communication disorders). Several of the special schools where I had previously worked encouraged staff to write in home/school diaries. This is a good traditional idea. However, writing messages is quite time-consuming, and it would be so much easier to be able to speak to parents on a daily basis. Staff from The Resource would be working on the move between classrooms and buildings. Messages and information could be given in much more detail and with more speed by using the spoken word.

Dictaphones now retail for between £15 and £20. These wonderful little machines appeared to be the home/school diary for the twenty-first century, and the one for us. They are easy to use and a better means of communication than the written word. They can be used with rechargeable batteries therefore keeping the cost down. For some of our parents, these little machines have proved to be a lifeline. Some parents are very stressed when their son/daughter starts at the school. They might view sending their child to a mainstream secondary school as a huge risk. In the first few weeks, listening to their messages on the dictaphone can take a long time. During the first few terms, it is interesting to hear the dictaphone messages getting increasingly shorter. We take this as a sign that anxiety levels are reducing. The dictaphone has played a role in this process. Some of our older pupils do not like the dictaphone because they see it as teachers and parents 'ganging up' on them. The dictaphone is then taken out of use for that individual. However, in the early terms, when a pupil is new and parents are understandably anxious, these little machines prove to be invaluable. When a pupil is going through a difficult time, the dictaphones can be a great source of comfort as parents moan to school staff and vice versa. The good times then become much sweeter as congratulatory messages pass between home and school. In the seven years of using these small and appealing tape machines, we have never had one stolen, although they can break. Their shelf life is about three years. Our record is a life of five years for two dictaphones.

We had no input from the services of a speech and language therapist for our first two years. This was a battle I was not expecting. In my naivety I thought that because we would be taking pupils with severe communication disorders, weekly input from a speech and language therapist would be provided. Nothing is ever that simple, even though the person in charge of this valuable service was on the interview panel when I got the position of teacher in charge. Area health authorities manage the service of speech and language therapy and they needed to know who was going to pay the bill. While it is very clear on all of the Statements of our pupils that speech and language therapy is required, it never states exactly how much. Statements are legal documents and so this should not have surprised me. With letters and meetings over the first two years, we achieved the services of a superb speech and language therapist for one half-day a week. Much of her time has to be taken with assessment for annual reviews, but the amount of therapy work has steadily increased over the years.

The number of meetings after school that occur in mainstream secondary education astounded me. There were management meetings, which include all heads of departments, pastoral meetings, department meetings, full staff meetings, and year team meetings. I had come from a small special school where we had a staff meeting each week at lunchtime. I observed these mainstream teachers work incredibly hard during the day, only to find them sitting in meetings, sometimes twice a week, until 5pm. Most of what we have achieved over the last six years has been grounded in two things: naivety and common sense. If pupils with ASD were to 'gain a voice' in this school, staff had to have a presence at all these meetings. To achieve a good model of inclusion, staff working with pupils who have any kind of additional need require a very high profile in the school. During my first term, I sat in on all the meetings. I went to various department meetings because these were new to me. The level of problem solving and debate I witnessed was of a very high standard. My mainstream colleagues, while being very human, were also incredibly businesslike. Deadlines had to be met for something or other almost every week of the year. Parents' meetings and social events such as concerts and poetry evenings added to the time these teachers spent at work.

I am not suggesting that colleagues in mainstream education work harder than those in the special sector. The pressures are different, as anybody who has worked in both sectors will know. However, the perception of a majority of mainstream teachers is that their colleagues in the special sector have a pretty easy life. This attitude was met in many of the classrooms I visited in that first term. To the uninitiated, supporting two or three pupils in a class of 30 has got to appear a relatively easy task, simply on a numerical basis. Somehow, we needed to prove to mainstream teachers that staff in The Resource worked as hard as, if not harder than, they did. We would not only have to have a high profile in school, but would have to learn about the requirements of every curriculum area (for each year group) so that we could at least speak the same language as mathematicians, scientists, graphic designers and food technology teachers. We would have to ensure that staff in The Resource would not be overlooked when it came to receiving agendas and minutes for meetings. In every sense, staff would have to fight for the right to be accepted, trusted and respected. We would have to integrate successfully with our colleagues alongside the pupils we would bring into the school.

Initially, the problems seemed numerous and insurmountable. Good models of access and inclusion are not achieved overnight. Only now, seven years into the journey, do I consider the school to be almost an inclusive setting for pupils with ASD. Lessons have to be learnt in the real-life setting for pupils and staff. Again, there are no magical shortcuts. Some of our mainstream colleagues took several years to get used to the idea of having another adult in the room. Credibility has to be earned. In subjects such as technology, the simple fact of relearning how to use a pillar drill and sanding machine took me a long time. Nudges and non-verbal jokes are still passed between technology teachers about the quality of my tongue and groove joints in woodwork. Building this number of relationships with teachers is extremely draining. There are those you can have a laugh with and those you cannot; those who make you cringe with their methods of discipline and those you want to yell at to 'get a grip' of the situation. The way Resource staff relate has to alter from hour to hour depending on which teacher they are supporting. The turnover of staff in a mainstream secondary school can be large, so the whole process is continually repeating itself. Adaptations to policy and practice have to be made 'on the run'. High profiles have to be maintained over several years, and this is draining on staff time. There is little respite. Mainstream pupils deserve the opportunity to increase their understanding of autism. Ideally, they need to reach the point where human differences are celebrated rather than made fun of.

The two pupils we began with in September 1994 were in every sense our guinea pigs. They taught us so much about inclusion. They helped to formulate future ideas and priorities. We made most of our mistakes with these two pupils, but they lived to tell the tale. In some respects they got a poor deal because The Resource base (i.e. all the building work) was not completed until eight weeks into their first term. They had nowhere to relax or escape from the incredible pressure we were putting them under. They are still our pioneers to this day. We did expect too much from them and our expectations were ridiculously high. It is to their credit (and the support they received from parents) that both pupils lived up to and surpassed these expectations.

However, there were some extremely difficult moments during their first term. One pupil had highly entertaining thoughts in his head and giggled out loud in class. This was difficult for him to control and uncomfortable for staff support- ing him, his mainstream peers and the subject teacher. On one occasion I had experienced a particularly stressful day with him. He had giggled uncontrollably throughout several lessons and my stress levels were through the roof. We were in a wonderful history lesson with one of the best teachers in the school. History was one of the many strengths of this pupil, but if we had had a base to go back to, I would have taken him there long before the major crisis – a crisis which was mine and not his. After several minutes of loud laughter while the history teacher attempted to explain the intricacies of Roman life in Britain, my patience snapped. My pupil was small at the time so I picked him up, put him under my arm and carried him out of the classroom. I am not proud of this and I certainly created some fear in the mind of this wonderful boy. The shock waves from my action affected the teacher and peers of this pupil. History remained one of his favourite lessons and over the years the uncontrolled laughter largely subsided. He also achieved a D grade at GCSE in history. I am not sure who was most proud, the student or the three wonderful history teachers he had over a five-year period.

Unfortunately, PE was a difficult subject for these first two pupils. Lots of movement and noise, whether inside or out, did appear to be difficult for them to manage. One pupil always seemed to end up in goal when it was football. If his opponents kicked the ball too hard, he would simply get out of the way or cover his face with his hands. This did little for his credibility, as the ball seemed to end up in the net on many occasions. Accidents always happen, but we have learnt that their outcome does not always have to be negative. As one particularly fiercely contested game moved into its final minute, the two sides were evenly matched at four goals each. Passion levels were running at maximum. A groan was heard (probably from me) as the opposition's best striker moved forward to confront our brave pupil who was shaking in the middle of the goal. As the biggest pupil in the class and the best footballer, he struck the ball with accuracy and venom. It hit our lad on the shoulder and rebounded wide of the goal. His first reaction was to cry in pain and frustration at his inability to dodge this particularly vicious shot. However, before he could scream his team mates were queuing up to congratulate him on such a fine save. Quickly picking up on the fact that this situation could work to his advantage, our lad dusted off his new and still pristine goalkeeping gloves and accepted this new-found adoration with good grace. I recall his main comment being, 'It's OK, I'm the goalkeeper, that's my job.' He was rarely on the winning team again, but this did not matter; in terms of PE, he had arrived.

Not all accidents have such a favourable outcome. Sticking with the lesson from hell, which PE can be on occasions, there was a water fountain in one of the changing rooms. This was used by most pupils to quench their thirst after a tough PE lesson. Early on in the first term, one of our pupils mistook this drinks fountain for a urinal. You can probably imagine the look of horror on my face as I turned to see him relieving himself in there. This did little to raise his self-esteem when he realised his genuine mistake. Equally, his credibility with pupils in his form inevitably suffered for a while. One of my friends, Andrew, has his story told in greater detail in Chapter 9.

Common sense prevailed with Mrs Smith, the head of sixth form, who had a healthy degree of scepticism about the relative merits of inclusion and access for our pupils. After several weeks of being bombarded with greetings and polite enquiries about her health, Mrs Smith knocked on my office door one morning.

'Mr Matthew,' she said (this is the name I use in school on account of having an unpronounceable surname) 'your children remind me of old-fashioned children. They are so polite and kind. I think things will be fine from now on.' And they were. Mrs Smith became a valued supporter of The Resource in her final year before retirement. The school and I miss her greatly.

The overriding feeling I had in those first two terms was a sense of the unique situation in which we found ourselves. Our staff team (which grew over the first five years) have never regarded themselves as theorists. We certainly read as many books as we could find, especially those written by people with autism or Asperger's syndrome. However, we were faced with having to act, not debate: we had to change things by actions, not words. Some adults with autism have written about the terrible time they experienced at mainstream secondary schools. While being very aware of this, we had an opportunity to make the experience of a mainstream secondary school a positive experience for our students. Few people, if any, were going to tell us how to do things in Sheffield, because nobody had done this before. We were on our own. This was both frightening and exhilarating. We had a chance to explore the highs and lows of integration, access and inclusion for pupils with ASD in a secondary school. Nobody was going to tell us something was impossible until we had first given it a go. No idea or plan would be deemed too difficult or expensive. If there was even the smallest chance of benefiting our pupils, we would give it a try: that remains the ethos right up to the present day. However, if I had known then what battles we would have to fight along the way, I would have run away to a safer and more secure job with great speed.

# 2

# The Key Players

A good model of access, integration and inclusion in a secondary school is dependent on three groups of people: the team of staff who support and enable; the mainstream subject teachers; the mainstream pupils. Each of these three groups has differing experiences, priorities and pressures. One ideal is to achieve all three groups planning and working together for the benefit of the pupils with autism. A further ideal is to illuminate the key issue that students with autism have much to teach all three groups of people about life, disability and the fact that being different in today's society is acceptable. As Gunilla Gerland (2000) writes: 'Being different is just as good as being like everyone else.'

Staffing ratios within integrated provisions have to be high. In most special schools that cater for pupils with ASD there will be one member of staff for every 2.5 pupils. This is certainly the case in most schools run by the National Autistic Society (NAS). Some pupils require one-to-one support. An integrated resource such as the one at King Ecgberts is no different. Inclusion cannot be achieved on the cheap. For the 20 pupils we support within the school, there are two teachers and six support workers, which is just about adequate. It was not achieved without struggle and sometimes we had to accept defeat. Every battle we had was to achieve the best possible support and environment for our pupils. Achieving an adequate staffing ratio was the biggest struggle for the first five years of our existence and occasionally we lost. In year three we had to lose a teacher and replace him with a support worker. During those five years we had to negotiate with three different officers who were in charge of special needs provision in Sheffield, which did not make the situation any easier. No written plan was in place concerning the increase in staffing over the first five years. The opportunities for disagreements between a teacher in charge of a growing resource in terms of pupil numbers and a principal officer of special needs are clear to see. We each had different aims and priorities. On occasions their overriding aim appeared to be a reduction in costs. One of our few safeguards was that the school would only permit four pupils a year who were statemented for severe communication disorders. This formed part of the initial agreement with the school. However, even in our second year there were more parents wanting places for their children than the four available. This situation appears to get worse with every year that passes.

In our second year we took four more pupils. Sheffield LEA very kindly advertised for one more teacher and support worker. This gave us six pupils with four staff. We needed them. I do not decide which pupils come to The Resource. There is a group of people called the Special Needs Panel who make these placement decisions based on the evidence they have at hand. One of the four pupils accepted in our second year worried me a great deal. Sean's autism was quite severe and I was not sure whether he would be happy in a mainstream school. My worries arose out of a genuine concern for his safety. He would be vulnerable to other pupils and it seemed to me and others that he would need the more protective environment offered by a good special school. The only person who thought this boy should attend a main-stream secondary school with support was his mother. This same student has just joined our post-16 provision. He experienced tremendous success in his social and academic life during five years at the school. Sean knew more people in the school than I did and was accepted and valued by the mainstream pupils in his form. He had a highly successful work placement with an insurance company for one morning a week over a three-year period. He missed a C grade in art GCSE by a miserly 1 per cent. (What are exam boards thinking of in these situations?) He was predicted to fail GCSE maths and got an F grade, as well as an E grade in food technology and IT. In return (not that staff needed it) Sean taught us all a great deal about autism and inclusion. Although I did not think we could do it, we got it right with Sean and inclusion was and continues to be a positive experience for him. I have yet to see Sean in the college environment, but I am told that he is calm, confident and happy. It is an experience he now rightly expects. In terms of admission into The Resource, his mother was right and I was very wrong.

If there are projects that fall outside the remit of education, this staffing ratio is not enough. If we were to push the boundaries back further in terms of access and inclusion, I knew that some of our plans for the future would be well outside the work we should be doing as educationalists. Some people admire our clumsy efforts into the world outside education. The LEA certainly found it difficult to understand and appreciate what we were doing and why. One type of this work will be discussed in Chapter 6.

Before The Resource existed, an increasing number of pupils with autism were being placed in secondary provisions outside Sheffield. An increasing number of parents were arguing and winning their cases to prove that there was no suitable provision for their sons/daughters within Sheffield. While The Resource cannot cater for all such pupils, we have taken some children who would have had to go outside Sheffield to receive appropriate education. From this point of view, integration can save money. The typical cost of a provision outside Sheffield that caters for pupils with ASD is approximately £40,000 per annum (which would be much higher if there were a residential element to the provision). Our cost per pupil is less than £9000 per annum, which is not cheap in terms of specialist education, but is also not expensive.

Staff coming into the team over the six years, including myself, have all had one thing in common: it has taken approximately a year to settle into the job. Integration and inclusion require a different type of thinking. Excellent support workers who were attracted to The Resource all state that they have never worked as hard as they do now. However, people will work hard if they can see good results. The ability to multi-task in what can appear to be a hostile environment for pupils with ASD is vital, but not easy. There are many 'layers' to doing the job well. Staff have to be a support and guide for the 20 pupils 'on our books'. They have to approach each situation within the framework of knowledge of autism, but with a mind that is continually open to new possibilities and approaches. They have to nurture and develop good relationships between our pupils and their mainstream peers. Pupils in the school who have an ASD have to be portrayed in a positive way, focusing on their individual strengths. However, the mainstream peers need to develop their understanding about children with disabilities, and communication disorders in particular. Each subject teacher is an individual and so Resource staff have to take time to build and foster good relationships with most of the 70 that work in the school. Tact, diplomacy and timing (i.e. knowing when to speak and when to bite your tongue) are skills needed in abundance. Building those essential links with parents is another facet to the job, which the dictaphones make easier.

Much of our working time is spent in isolation. When working with one or two pupils, a member of staff from The Resource is alone in the supportive role, which takes a very strong person. In addition, the supportive role is just that – you are not 'in charge'. The subject teacher is delivering the lesson. It is easy for staff to feel that they are second-class citizens in a school and this apparent lack of control is not something everyone can manage. However, staff in The Resource are part of a team. We see each other every day, we have our own department meetings and talk about subject teachers in our own safe environment. 'Sounding off' about difficult teachers or poor lessons is allowed and encouraged within the confines of The Resource. Communication skills, very often executed on the move, have to be circumspect.

We place two pupils with autistic spectrum disorders in a mainstream form of approximately 30 children. With an entry of four pupils, this gives staff two forms to work in from the first year. Initially, a member of staff from The Resource will support these two pupils in a form.

The first point to stress is that staff have to get to know the mainstream pupils in that form as well as they do the two children they are supporting. The member of staff becomes a valuable resource in that form. A mainstream subject teacher may see a particular form for two or maybe three hours a week. Resource staff will be with that form in their first term for 24 lessons a week. This means that we get to know who are the 'key players' in a form: the 'loveable rogues', the pupils who do not want to play any role and those who are open to learning more about their two classmates with an autistic spectrum disorder. Staff get to know the little cliques of pupils that develop and which groups are likely to have a greater tolerance towards the children we support. We can usually work out who has the potential to become a friend and who will be just acquaintances.

The personnel of the school quickly realised that we had potential in this area. Form tutors saw Resource staff as an asset, because they were in a better position to get to know the form than they were. Resource staff are an extra pair of hands at registration. We also experience a school day that is very different from that of the teachers since, in effect, our days are the same as the pupils'. It was recognised that we had a unique insight into what the school day was like from the pupils' point of view. Staff can explain why a particular class might be late to a lesson, because they were in the previous lesson which overran by five minutes. This also puts us in a different position in the eyes of the pupils. I do not mean this in a derogatory way, but staff from The Resource are seen not as teachers, but as ordinary human beings by the mainstream pupils. We have to suffer the 'slings and arrows' of the poor lessons as well as enjoy the vast majority of brilliant ones. Some mainstream pupils get to know staff from

The Resource better than any other adult in their school, which most of the time is a real bonus for us.

The team of staff in The Resource are superb for several reasons. They are all dedicated to providing a first-class, inclusive service to pupils with autistic spectrum disorders. They take pride in the fact that they are involved in work that is different and making a difference. They work harder and give more of their time than I have any right to ask. They celebrate the success of our pupils and support each other through tough times. This has not happened overnight.

Support workers are paid a much lower salary than teachers; in fact their salary levels are an insult. There is little career structure, which means that retention of excellent support workers is always difficult. Therefore, it has been vital for the support workers in The Resource to see the teacher in charge (i.e. me) do the same hands-on job that they do for most of the week. This suited me fine because I enjoy working with children much more than managing The Resource. Most of the extra work in managing The Resource has to go on behind the scenes. All staff in an educational environment need to feel that they have ownership of the work. This is the case in The Resource and we have some very strong characters within the team, which is always a positive factor. Nobody would do what I wanted if they disagreed. Staff feel comfortable and empowered enough to have their own say. This makes for stressful life as a manager, but there are no dull days. Each member of staff has to reach the point where he or she can put forward any idea if it is for the benefit of our pupils. However, when staff are confronted by a manager who 'dreams big', it takes time for them to share in this and believe that things will happen. Most workers in education are used to financial constraints and working within a system that usually develops at a snail's pace, if at all. Changes are not always for the best.

Initially, staff in The Resource had to listen to the soundings of a 'young upstart' who said that things were going to be different

– and quickly. I got approving nods and pats on the head in the first couple of years. Now, I am glad to say, staff are impatient for the next development to occur. The dreams are now theirs. Ownership of the development of The Resource has shifted from one person to many. Staff are making a great difference through their work, and now allow me a little time to put effort into enabling us to address the next problem. It is easy for staff in The Resource (especially after a difficult day) to think of moving into a safer and less demanding job.

Staff also have to witness me suffer and struggle with stressful situations. For example, in our second year there were questions asked about why we had no burglar alarm in The Resource. Sheffield LEA said that it was not their responsibility and the school should pay. The management of the school said that if they had to pay for an alarm (£300) The Resource would have to close because there should be no financial cost to them of having us as their guests. There have been many such incidents through the years when we have been caught between a rock and a hard place. The LEA eventually did pay for the alarm and the school was right to hold out for this. The team has had to manage with the continual threat of a reduction in staffing levels and the pressure at times has been immense. Reasoned arguments did not always win the day since The Resource is not supported by everyone in Sheffield. There have been times when I feel like a marked man. This apparent lack of control and continual uncertainty about the future are stresses that only a group of well-balanced and strong people can manage – The Resource is fortunate to be blessed with such a group of people.

What has been equally frustrating for support workers and teachers alike in The Resource has been the lack of training. The Resource has never had a training budget from Sheffield LEA. It took six years to persuade the school that they should give staff a training budget: £750 a year for eight staff does not provide much training. What can then be frustrating for staff is that when they do attend a training course they are seen as the experts on integration and inclusion for pupils with autistic spectrum disorders. On a recent training course the leader jokingly asked one of my colleagues if she was a spy. The Resource is not part of a large umbrella organisation such as the National Autistic Society. Despite our continual efforts, we have not been able to secure attendance on any of their superb courses at a reduced cost. For a society that purports to be 'national', it is worrying that all children with autism or Asperger's syndrome in mainstream education are outside their remit.

The role of the second teacher in The Resource is a 'nightmare'. First, the person has to cope with a 'driven' teacher in charge. Teachers have usually invested six years of their education in qualifying. The teaching role in The Resource is precious, but there are still large parts of the week spent in a role supportive to pupils and subject teachers. I have yet to find a teacher who enjoys this second-in-charge role and can do it well. Several have gone back to the safety of a special school or primary school where they can shut the classroom door and be 'in charge'. I do not blame them for this; not many teachers want to play this supportive role. Most quite rightly want to spend large parts of their week actually teaching. However, as one of our more able pupils put it, 'I don't want to be taught; all I need is a guide through the nightmare of teenage life'.

It is clear to me that the success of any inclusive education depends to a large extent on the mainstream pupils. At secondary age these thousands of hormonal teenagers from different backgrounds and cultures can be the proverbial pains in the rear, or your biggest supporters. It is made clear to parents of pupils with ASD that bullying and teasing occurs in all secondary schools. There are several strategies we employed from day one to make sure that the mainstream pupils, or the vast majority of them, were on our side.

In the first few weeks of their time at King Ecgbert School, the Year 7 pupils who have direct contact with children from The Resource receive information and guidance about communication disorders. This is delivered through their tutorial lesson (one lesson a week used to look at a variety of social issues). These lessons are great fun. There is little use in asking a group of Year 7 pupils if any of them have seen the film *Rainman* as it was made before they were born. What distresses me is that most of them have not heard of Dustin Hoffman. Games are played with these mainstream Year 7 pupils to highlight the fact that we all have communication difficulties. Videos are shown of very bright adults with autism to explode the idea that this disability denotes a learning deficit. 'Word throws' are used to try to illuminate the fact that deriving meaning from a sentence is a complicated process if you 'miss' any of the information. For example, the sentence 'stand behind your chair and stick your fingers in your ears' is cut up as single words on card and weighted with a penny stuck on the back. An explanation is then given to the pupils that it is difficult to understand and derive meaning from language if you miss the meanings of some words, or take a little longer to process them. The handful of single words is then gently thrown towards one of the unsuspecting pupils with the instruction to 'catch'. Only words that are caught can be used to make the sentence. Any words that drop to the floor cannot be used. I have had children cleaning their ears, standing on chairs and looking behind the ears of other pupils – all great fun, but it does seem to get the idea across about disability and language.

Cards are shown with pictures of people from different cultures and backgrounds on them. The pupils split into small groups to look at a card with six or seven pictures of people on it. They are given the task of picking out the person who has a communication disorder. The ideas and rationale flow back and forth, but most groups usually come up with one or two people who they think might be 'the ones'. When I explain that I have no idea which of these people, if any, has a communication disorder, the groans are music to my ears. (For some reason I do not understand, one of the faces continually picked as a person who might have a communication disorder was a famous local footballer in

Sheffield.) Plenty of time is left for questions. The message is given loud and clear that the two pupils in their form who have an autistic spectrum disorder are *not* their responsibility, but it does not take a second to say 'hello'.

These lessons are enjoyable, but they are no substitute for experiencing real lessons and making use of real-life opportunities. One of our pupils did not get off to a very good start with the mainstream peers in his form. He desperately wanted some friends but could not quite find the right approaches. He invaded their personal space and repeatedly used the phrase 'Hello, how are you?' This is a good phrase, but not when used to the same person 20 times a day. Fortunately, during one of the first IT lessons, this boy was able to shine at something. While I was occupied supporting another pupil, I looked up to see about ten children surrounding Jordan and the computer he was using. More were drifting across to see what was happening. With a feeling of dread in my stomach, I ran over. Jordan was typing on the keyboard. I knew from his notes that his typing skills were good, but he was very fast. Oblivious to the scene he had caused, Jordan carried on typing at great speed, while his mainstream peers stood and watched with their mouths wide open in disbelief. They had listened and participated in the tutorial about autism, but now they were seeing first hand one of the points I had tried (in vain) to get across. These same pupils now respect Jordan for some of his skills. They also support him in the things he is not so good at. On sports day Jordan was determined to do the 100-metre sprint. He was never going to win and would be lucky to finish the short distance, as running was not one of his strengths. The race was over and won as Jordan was just setting off, but the cheers and yells of encouragement from friends in his form brought a tear to the most hardened eye.

The tutorial lessons will never be enough to enable mainstream pupils to develop a good understanding of autism. Other strategies have developed over time. The question most asked by parents who are looking at The Resource as a potential secondary place for their son or daughter is about bullying in the school. All schools will say they have a good and effective policy for dealing effectively with bullying, but it still goes on. What we see in schools is only a reflection of what is happening in society. King Ecgbert School has bullying boxes where pupils can leave confidential information about unpleasant incidents. The school has quite a good pastoral system and a wonderful deputy head who seems to deal with most difficult situations between pupils.

With our high profile in school, staff work closely with 'problem pupils'. Incidents are picked up quickly and further discussions occur with these pupils on a one-to-one basis. As The Resource base is open at lunchtime, we do see a number of pupils who have a wide range of additional needs. The hope is that they see The Resource as a place where they do not have to tease or bully other pupils. Generally, they have respected staff and the fact that we do let them into our area at lunchtimes. With staff being close to some of these difficult pupils, we are in a position to listen and advise. One boy was having great problems in his friendship with a pupil from The Resource. After several discussions, he confided to me that he had always had difficulty controlling his temper and it worried him a great deal. He did not want to turn out like his father. We were able to talk about some basic anger management as well as how he could improve his relationships with other people, especially those with whom he found it hard to get on. Integration and inclusion has to be viewed as a two-way process. We expect other people to 'give' to us through increased understanding and awareness. It should be expected that other people, mainstream pupils for example, might sometimes need our support.

In terms of pupils who bring their problems into school, along with their maths and French books, staff can only scratch the surface of the huge difficulties they face. Sometimes we see a glimpse of progress. A particularly difficult character was in the same form as one of our most severely autistic lads. He listened to the tutorial lesson and additional explanations about autism and how vulnerable this particular pupil from The Resource could be. One lunchtime, he proudly strutted into The Resource and announced that he had seen some other pupils who did not understand about autism victimising his friend Sean. When I enquired about the incident and which pupils I should talk to, he reassured me that this would not be necessary. It was his belief that they would never trouble Sean again. I realised that it was perhaps wiser to ask no further questions. These pupils never did tease Sean again, and this 'difficult character' and I became firm friends. He treated Sean and me with respect and friendship over the next four years.

Activities that occur in a school can often bring staff, Resource and mainstream pupils much closer together. The annual 13-mile sponsored walk is one such activity. There is little that unites people and develops their understanding of each other better than the sharing of an activity which causes physical pain. Concerts at Christmas and the end of the academic year are wonderful opportunities for pupils from The Resource to be up there performing on stage with everyone else. The school has a good drama department and this area gives our pupils further opportunities to demonstrate the positive side of integration. Sporting activities also present opportunities to follow the interests of a pupil and assist in the process of challenging notions about disability. One of our pupils became a good cross-country runner. Sometimes inclusion entails spending a freezing cold and rainy day in winter cheering on runners from King Ecgbert's, but in particular the pupil from The Resource. These occasions are also tremendous events for parents to witness. They offer the opportunity for parents to be proud; parents need to feel proud of their children. Other pupils have taken part in extra-curricular activities such as football and athletic clubs after school. Staff have remained after school time to support these pupils until they can gain some independence.

Mainstream teachers in secondary schools have an extremely difficult job, and not one that I would either want or be good at.

With the sheer number of pupils the average subject teacher sees in one week, the range of academic ability to be catered for, the quantity of marking and administrative tasks, the number of meetings and the poor working environments in many of our crumbling schools, they have my complete admiration. It is also not surprising that many of our mainstream colleagues in the school began with some strange notion that working with pupils who have some kind of additional need is a 'cushy number'.

The fact that staff from The Resource covered all the variety of meetings in school helped to integrate the staff. Good teachers celebrate success. The majority of our pupils are experiencing success both academically and socially, witnessed by our mainstream colleagues. They are quick to point out when a pupil has achieved something for the first time. Teachers have seen at first hand how much effort a pupil from The Resource is willing to put into a subject if the supportive environment is correct.

The mainstream teachers who work with pupils from The Resource see the support staff at least once a week in their lessons. This point of contact has to be kept. Questions, misunderstandings, good and not so good lessons can all be discussed there and then. Most teachers are now very aware that they have to warn the pupils or staff of any forthcoming alterations to lessons. Some teachers come to The Resource during non-contact periods to have a coffee and see how we are doing, which is always appreciated.

The management of the school now treat The Resource just as they do any other department. We have to produce annual development plans and discuss them with a member of the management team. The Resource is 'inspected' by the senior management team in the same way as the English, maths and science departments. I am just another head of department. This has taken seven years, but I think we have arrived.

However, each new academic year brings changes in personnel. Teachers leave and new ones come in their place. The process of inclusion and education about autism is ongoing and never ending. New teachers to the school have a lunchtime meeting with me to introduce them to the ideas and philosophy of integration, inclusion and The Resource.

All GCSEs have some coursework content today. Given that this coursework is done well following criteria laid down by the examination boards, a pupil can take a good grade into the final exams. For some GCSEs, especially technology, the coursework can contribute as much as 60 per cent to the final grade. One of our less academically able pupils was interested in attempting the textiles GCSE. The coursework consists of planning, research, design and evaluation of whatever the pupil decides to make: in Tom's case, a sports bag. To achieve consistent and expert support, one member of staff from The Resource volunteered to take this role on for the required two years. The amount of work was immense and a lot had to be carried out in Resource lessons. The project and the sports bag were completed and the grade given by the textiles teacher was a D.

Equalling this grade in the written paper with this pupil would be miraculous. Exam techniques had to be taught and the type of question that occurred regularly on the paper had to be studied. In one question, pupils would have to suggest the most suitable material for a given purpose. Tom became a little over-interested in leather as the best material for all purposes. It was not unusual for him to suggest leather as the most appropriate material for curtains, bedclothes, sleeping bags and tents. Over the months, curtaining, children's play tents and sleeping bags were brought in to demonstrate materials which might be slightly more appropriate than leather. Tom enjoyed learning all of this, especially concerning the tent and sleeping bag in which he promptly fell asleep. He kept his D grade in the final exam, supported by my wonderful colleague who had travelled with him on the two-year GCSE textiles journey. The textiles teacher played her part with Tom and the Resource staff member. I am confident that she took as much pleasure from Tom's D grade as she did from those pupils who achieved an A grade.

This experience has been replicated in food and art GCSEs. Each new year sees our pupils branching into GCSEs in which staff have no experience: we will soon have pupils doing GCSEs in PE, media studies and resistant materials. These subject teachers will see our pupils and The Resource staff putting tremendous effort and teaching into their GCSEs.

At its best, inclusion should be the sharing of knowledge and experience between the specialist and mainstream sectors of education. Numbers count in the secondary education system of today. Teachers are praised for how many students get A to C passes at GCSE. Schools receive praise if they get results that are higher than the national average. Staff from The Resource had to accept this from day one. We have to know when to 'shout' about individual pupils and when to 'sit on our hands'. However, the majority of teachers take pride and pleasure in pupils who strive to do their very best. These individuals will receive the credit and praise from teachers they so rightly deserve and are what most teachers joined the profession for. Teachers would place most pupils from The Resource in this group. A small minority will get A to C grades at GCSE, but most will be working for that D or E grade. Teachers can see that this is only possible with expert support, guidance and sheer hard work. Through such efforts The Resource staff have become increasingly accepted by the majority of their mainstream colleagues. There are no short cuts.

Training with our mainstream colleagues was not attempted until the fifth year. Any sooner would not have been appropriate because we were not ready to speak and they were not ready to listen. It took five years of dedication on the part of Resource staff to convince some of our mainstream colleagues that our work was not an easy option. Some nuts are harder to crack than others. There were several different strategies that seemed to work well. With our first two pupils, integration was achieved on a written contract basis. This contract was signed and accepted by the teacher, member of staff from The Resource and the parents. An example of such a contract is shown in Figure 2.1.

# Record of Integration

**Name**:            Terry Jones

**Form**:             7LH

**Subject**:        History

**Teacher**:        Mr Happy

**Level of integration**: Two lessons a week.

**Purpose of integration**:

1. To gain information/learning about Roman Britain.
2. To experience good models of social communication in the lesson.
3. To gain some acceptance from his peers in a subject which is a strength area for Terry.

**Agreed length of integration:** One term

**Criteria for success:**

1. Terry to be enjoying history lessons.
2. Mr Happy to be more confident in his relationship with Terry.
3. Terry to be less reliant on support from Resource staff.

**Review by**:           December 1994.

If you have any difficulties/questions or suggestions concerning this pupil, please do not hesitate to talk to a member of staff from The Resource.

***Signed and copies to:*** Parents, mainstream teacher, resource staff.

*Figure 2.1 Record of integration*

This apparently insignificant sheet of paper turned out to serve a useful purpose. Mainstream teachers felt that they had some say in the process of integration. They were active in the process rather than passive. They could see what we were attempting to do and that we could not succeed without them. The record helped to establish a channel of communication between the mainstream teachers and Resource staff. However, for two pupils each integrating into nine subject areas, the prospect of mountains of paperwork was not pleasing. Having to complete these sheets for each pupil once a term and then evaluate them was never going to be a viable option. One term into our first year, we had developed and nurtured some degree of trusting relationships with 'our' group of mainstream teachers. This agreement about integration and its purpose would subsequently be achieved through verbal contracts. Excessive and useless paperwork must be avoided.

When it did occur, training was well planned and well received. Staff wanted the training to be informative, but fun. We wanted the mainstream teachers to remember the message and the evening itself. We did the training for one-half of the teachers at a time (about 35). One colleague introduced the session and gave instructions to the teachers about how to make an origami bird. Paper and scissors were given to the mainstream subject teachers. Other colleagues from our team sat with them and also made the folded paper birds. Two Resource staff walked around the classroom being very strict with the unruly element one always gets when a group of teachers is placed in a room. The difficulty for the teachers was that the instructions on how to make the bird were given in a mixture of English and Welsh, creating utter confusion. Some teachers began to look to staff from The Resource who were completing the task with apparent ease. This was a good idea and one that our pupils employ in the classroom. However, any modelling was quickly pounced on with reminders that they should listen more carefully to the instructions given by the teacher at the front. One teacher had to be sent out of the room for disrupting the lesson. It really was great fun, and provided opportunities for follow-up discussions about pupils with severe communication disorders. Teaching tips about using visual materials, keeping instructions clear and concise, checking to ensure a pupil has understood what is expected of him/her and being careful about the use of humour and sarcasm became much easier to get across. It also enabled us to get some excellent feedback about the service we provide. Staff were split into smaller groups to discuss the 'good, bad and ugly' factors of having The Resource in the school. This was overwhelmingly positive, but also included some areas upon which we could improve. The disadvantages included:

- some behaviour of Resource pupils disrupts the classroom and other pupils may feel they are 'getting away with it'
- peculiar incidents in class
- pupils can demand a lot of time and attention if there is no support
- demands on teaching strategies: i.e. having to be primarily visual rather than verbal, can be demanding in terms of preparation time
- resource staff talking in lessons when the teacher is giving instructions
- support can emphasise 'differences' to the rest of the class
- staff not really aware of the current 'mind set' of a Resource pupil
- difficult for the teacher to personalise all instructions for Resource pupils in the class
- difficult to do anything unplanned or unexpected in lessons

- working on a one-to-one basis might isolate the Resource pupil from his/her peers
- when support is present, it is easy for the subject teacher to overlook the pupil from The Resource

The positives of having The Resource in the school included:

- encouraging good understanding of autism from other people
- access to good models of communication
- having another adult in the room
- thinking more carefully about giving instructions
- increased awareness of other 'special needs' pupils who would benefit from better teaching
- for autistic children in Sheffield, The Resource is somewhere specialised and mainstream for them to go
- the appreciation of seeing pupils with difficulties coping and making such fantastic progress
- the Resource pupils' 'condition' is *not* seen as excluding them from classroom activities
- provides information for teachers to call on
- provides a safe haven for 'non-Resource' pupils at lunchtime
- useful for other pupils to realise that disability does not have to involve wheelchairs, hearing aids, etc.
- Resource pupils need and receive intensive support
- presents challenges for other students – a Resource pupil doing very well in a subject may stimulate other pupils to try harder to overcome their own difficulties
- presence of support staff around school generally – Resource staff add a very positive dimension to the whole school

- immense sense of achievement when 'the penny drops' for pupil and teacher
- we know there is someone to understand and support the pupil.

This feedback gave Resource staff something concrete to discuss in department meetings. New ways of working are continually being developed and tried to see if we can improve our service to pupils and mainstream teachers.

The vast majority of teachers were a joy to work with from day one. One of our pupils became very interested in baldness. We timetabled this interest to occur within the safety of The Resource and looked at the great bald men in history, politics and sport. We assumed that the situation was under control with a great deal of skill and effort from our team until the maths lesson on Friday afternoon. As I sat beside this same pupil, he became increasingly agitated and finally put up his hand. The teacher, a wonderful man, gave Shaun the opportunity to speak. In a very clear and loud voice Shaun told the teacher that, in his opinion, his bald patch had grown larger since the last maths lesson. Shaun's mainstream peers collapsed in heaps of laughter, and very little maths work was undertaken in the remainder of that lesson. The teacher was quick to realise that Shaun meant no harm by this comment; it was, after all, just an observation. The thought was there and so it had to be articulated. He remains one of our greatest supporters, and I his.

One of our tasks is continually to encourage pupils to become more independent. Over-dependence on our support was something we were worried about from the beginning. With full support being given over the first half-term for most pupils to get a good 'foundation', independence had to be kept uppermost in our minds as soon as it was appropriate. Initially, this was not easy to achieve with some mainstream teachers because of the pressure they were under. Staff from The Resource support one to three pupils in a lesson. In a class of 30, there might be four or five other pupils with some kind of additional need. More able pupils who are doing extension activities might want to ask questions. Some teachers agreed that the pupils from The Resource did not need further support. However, they appreciated that our role in their class was much wider than this, and did not want us to leave because their job would become more difficult. This was problematic for staff who were becoming increasingly knowledgeable about subject areas and the stresses inherent in mainstream teaching. However, we had to be strong and argue the case for independence for our pupils.

The level of independence varies from one pupil to another, in different year groups and over the course of the academic year. However, generally speaking, the level of independence in lessons increases for all pupils as the academic year progresses. Some of our pupils in Years 7, 8 or 10 could expect to be independent for approximately one-third of their weekly timetable by Easter. Support has to be higher during Year 9 because of SATS and during Year 11 because of coursework and GCSEs. Independence does not have to cover a full lesson; it can be for half an hour or 20 minutes. We would rarely give a pupil full independence in any one subject. This is because staff have to have some presence in a subject in order to keep up to date with the teaching, homework and coursework requirements. Independence is not just about lessons, but can include crossing the road between buildings, or using public transport to and from school. The overwhelming majority of pupils see independence from Resource staff as a good thing and a sign that they are making progress.

There will always be the odd one or two teachers out of a staff of over 70 who simply do not like having pupils with ASD in their classroom and dislike having another adult with them even more. There will always be the odd one or two teachers who give the impression that they do not really like children. I overheard a worker in a supermarket comment recently that his job is great apart from the customers. There are few answers to this difficulty; I guess it is just part of life. I can only point to the tremendous pressure under which mainstream teachers work, and try to understand. Wherever possible, we avoid placing pupils with ASD in these difficult classes. However, it can become virtually impossible when mainstream pupils expect Resource staff to do something about the 'teacher from hell'. As they rightly point out, we saw what that teacher did, or heard the way in which s/he spoke to them. We would never comment in a negative manner about any teacher to the management of the school. It is way outside our role and would destroy any trust built up with teachers in the school. However, we can suggest that mainstream pupils who feel unfairly treated should speak to their parents. Parents can then make representation to the school. Ask any mainstream pupils about which teachers they genuinely dislike and they will come up with a list of one or two.

One of the kindest things a mainstream colleague said to me recently was that the establishment of The Resource was the best thing that had happened to the school in the last 15 years. Some of the first mainstream pupils we worked alongside still return to visit The Resource and its staff. These young adults recognised that Resource staff were human beings at a time when this was a difficult role to play in schools. We witnessed the highs and lows of their teenage years without judgement. They supported and encouraged the two pupils in their form. Everyone won.

Now that we are having success with our post-16 students (see Chapter 8), it is a source of pride for mainstream teachers that they share in this. I can almost read their minds and see them thinking (quite rightly) that they have played a role in the process – they too are beginning to help push back the boundaries for pupils with ASD. They are beginning to share and take ownership of the dream.

# 3

# Parents, Paperwork and Pressure

In the first term of The Resource, the school was visited by OFSTED (the government's inspectors of schools). I sat in my office/drama cupboard and tried to tell one of the inspectors about how The Resource would develop and progress over the next five years. There were no pupils for him to observe in lessons and no packages of learning in place, but he went away confused and happy. The visit underlined one of the pressures we felt from day one: people wanted us to tell them about our work before we had started.

Every job carries pressure that others can find difficult to comprehend. Our pressure came from several sources, the main one being that we were making it up as we went along. There were no guidebooks or fountains of wisdom to which we could refer. Nobody had any precise answers for us. On a good day this pressure is called excitement. On a difficult day – and there have been plenty over the last seven years – the prospect of producing a new idea, working on a unique plan, battling with the LEA or just going into a lesson you know will be tough, can leave staff feeling isolated, tired or simply fed up. The everyday role of teacher, support, counsellor, social secretary, and friend can be draining when staff are tired or feel under pressure.

From the first year of our existence the telephone rang on a regular basis with calls from other secondary schools wanting advice on pupils with autism or Asperger's syndrome. Sheffield now had its very own fountain of wisdom called The Resource.

This was and still is the most challenging aspect which staff have to confront. Visits were booked to talk to other schools in Sheffield about autism. Staff in these schools often wanted specific advice, which was difficult to offer without first observing the pupil in question. This role became a part of the job and took up a lot of time. We were not ready to talk and yet staff in schools had few other people to turn to. Materials had to be produced quickly to support this work. These talks took place after the school day had finished. Centres of training for teachers wanted talks about autism and our work. This type of work has increased steadily over the seven years of The Resource's existence.

People from other local education authorities wanted to visit The Resource as soon as it opened its doors to the first two pupils and the quantity of visitors has increased steadily. Recently, members of the team took the difficult decision of preventing visitors from coming to The Resource until after the first few months of a new academic year. Most people are very understanding about this. I am never quite sure what to show visitors anyway. The most important resource in any educational establishment is the people who make up the team of staff. They just look like anybody else. Once the introductions have been made, what else does one say? Some visitors become uncomfortable when they are taken into a classroom 'out of the way'. Yet, staff have to get on with their work. Integration and inclusion should look 'normal' and there is not a great deal to see going on in lessons. We do not use 'boxes' to screen off our pupils from their peers. Screening out unwanted sounds and sights can be difficult for some of our pupils, but the problems caused by putting some kind of box around their desk would be much greater. Inclusion must never be only about the two pupils we have in a mainstream lesson of maths, for example; it has as much to do with the other 28 pupils in the maths lesson and the teacher as well. But you cannot show that to a visitor in any real sense. Besides, should we really be allowing visitors to peer through the windows of the maths classroom as if inclusion is something extraordinary?

The pressure was on to write learning packages for use in The Resource once we realised that nothing already published would suit the needs of our pupils. The life skills and personal and social education (PSE) packages are discussed in greater detail in Chapter 5.

In terms of learning and cognitive skills, the pressure arises from striking the correct balance between a mainstream and a specialist curriculum geared to the needs of individual pupils. Mainstream has to be the focus of our attention and efforts, but this will never be enough for any of the Resource pupils. Special schools themselves are under great pressure to adhere to the national curriculum. This must prove extremely difficult for schools that cater for pupils with profound and multiple disabilities. I would always question the validity of teaching a modern foreign language to a pupil in a wheelchair who has great difficulties with any kind of speech or comprehension of language. To teach the same pupil the intricacies of the rise to power of communism in Soviet Russia, or the effects of economic depression in the USA in the 1930s would appear to be a long way removed from trying to make the curriculum fit the needs of that person.

The same is true for pupils with ASD. DJ absolutely loathed history and the two weekly history lessons caused more difficulties than all the other subjects put together. We encouraged DJ to persevere with history for two and a half years. It was clear that he would rather be burned at the stake than opt for history as a GCSE subject. At the Year 8 parents' evening, his mother, accompanied by her son, approached the history teacher with some trepidation. The conversation between mother and teacher was polite and honest. DJ as usual stole the moment by cutting through all the niceties and talking directly about the issue with his history teacher. His comment was that while the teacher was brilliant at his job, it was no fault of his that he had to deliver the most boring subject on the curriculum. Teacher and pupil emerged from the consultation with respect for each other intact.

There are many examples of staff in The Resource making decisions about the mainstream curriculum of individual pupils. No pupil does all ten GCSEs. For pupils who have the potential to attain the higher A to C grades, there is little point in attempting ten subjects when only five such passes are required to access higher qualifications. One pupil in The Resource adores modern foreign languages and also has some skills in them. He opted to continue with French and German at GCSE. However, most of our pupils do not attempt a second modern foreign language when the national curriculum states they have to at Year 8. I have yet to be convinced of the validity of Resource pupils spending up to four hours a week learning modern foreign languages. Staff in The Resource could use two of these hours much more appropriately teaching communication, life and PSE skills. With our pupils beginning to have input into their own curriculum, staff need to create time to satisfy these individual requirements. These may range from trips out of school with related project work, exploring areas of life they have questions about, or learning how to use public transport.

Some of our pupils do not enjoy the technology subjects. With little enjoyment, there is not usually a great deal of learning occurring either. In such areas, if staff were to insist on attendance the mainstream pupils might see someone with autism at their least cooperative. This will not assist with inclusive attitudes or tolerance levels. It will probably not be vital for the future employment prospects or personal development of the individual pupil to study a technology subject. Yet the national curriculum insists that all pupils should opt for at least one technology subject at GCSE. Most pupils from The Resource are encouraged to abide by this rule, but only if the price is worth paying. If the price is too high in terms of self-esteem, the pupil will not opt for a technology subject. Each pupil tries the different subjects within the technology curriculum for three years anyway, so why persevere for a further two with little or no gain in terms of personal development, social interaction or cognitive skills?

Pressure is the inevitable cost of such decisions. Devising a curriculum to satisfy the needs of individual pupils necessitates moving outside the confines of the national curriculum, and therefore a little outside the law as it stands at present. The national curriculum has much to offer the majority of pupils, but one model can never meet the needs of all children. However, to step outside the accepted norms and current wisdom leaves staff open to criticism that they are not providing a 'well-rounded' education, whatever that is. This brings us back to the pressure/excitement of making it up as we go along. I would rather view this invention as making the curriculum suit the needs of individual pupils. Within the confines of a mainstream school, staff have to strive continually to focus on the needs of the individual pupil. Once this focus is lost, children are forced to fit into the model of an existing curriculum.

After four years, the OFSTED inspectors returned to the school. The pressure of a full OFSTED inspection is well documented. The amount of preparation for inspection must not be underestimated since it can determine the future reputation of a school. The stress placed on staff and school management is immense. We were no different. In fact, for staff in The Resource the pressure was greater because we knew that we were doing things a little differently. We were fortunate enough to meet a very understanding and forward thinking inspector. He gave the impression of listening and wanting to learn about the ways in which we were trying to work with our pupils. Instead of the sharp intake of breath we were expecting, we received warm words of encouragement. He looked with interest at lesson plans on prostitution, homosexuality and sexual aids that we had in our PSE package. He did not frown at the fact that our pupils were missing out on RE lessons and instead offered advice about how we could justify what we were teaching as an alternative to the National Curriculum. We were apologetic, and he persuaded us to be proud. The direct comments made about The Resource in the final report are shown in Figure 3.1. They are not included to persuade the reader how wonderful The Resource is, but rather to gain encouragement that people can do things differently and be rightly praised for doing so.

## OFSTED inspection

'Many [pupils] are working with much less adult support than would have been expected if they had been placed in a school for pupils with such special needs.'

'One Year 8 pupil was successful in working through an entire top set maths lesson with no additional support.'

'They [the pupils] make good progress, for example in learning to use public transport, shop and use the telephone through a programme of graded steps.'

'Pupils show a very positive attitude towards their education.'

'The support given by staff is good and often very good.'

'Relationships are excellent and high levels of trust are established in order to create an ethos where pupils feel safe to develop.'

[The] 'combination of staff from The Resource and the school works to the best advantage of the pupils.'

'The curriculum is very carefully constructed and is supported by materials developed by the team.'

'All the staff have a high profile throughout the mainstream school and bring considerable expertise which is valued by parents.'

'The Resource provides excellent value for money in providing very positive educational outcomes for pupils with severe communication disorders within the 11 to 16 range.'

*Figure 3.1 OFSTED inspection*

Pressure comes in great waves from one sad but true fact. There is not enough quality provision in education, tertiary or adult services for people with autistic spectrum disorders. There are not enough provisions and the range is not wide enough to encompass all people with autism. The Resource at King Ecgbert School in Sheffield can cater for four pupils a year. We can cater for those children who it is felt might benefit in some way from experience of a mainstream curriculum and a mainstream environment with some support. The fact that the choice facing parents at the secondary stage of education in Sheffield is either a special school, King Ecgbert or an out-of-city placement is not acceptable. The Resource cannot cater for all children on the spectrum. We cannot accommodate all those children who should have access to a mainstream secondary school.

On average, 20 sets of parents each year want to come and look at The Resource to see if it would be appropriate for their son/daughter. On our last open evening for parents, two people travelled over a hundred miles to see The Resource. Parents who do not live in the city of Sheffield want to come and see The Resource. Parents of children in other secondary schools require services specific to their needs and think that staff at The Resource hold the answers. Being approached to get involved in family therapy or respite care is very flattering, but it is a source of anger that these services are so underfunded that pupils and their families are waiting years to receive anything appropriate. We have had to watch students fail, and begin to show signs of depression, while waiting for appropriate services to be delivered by external agencies such as social services.

We are also under some pressure to accept people involved in research concerning the area of autism. One researcher doing her PhD was with us for an average of one day a week for over eighteen months. However, this piece of research was well worth it and it was a privilege for The Resource to be involved. Sometimes the requests for visits appear a little alternative even for us, but it is difficult to turn people down. Given that we are constantly searching for solutions and possible ways forward, how can we turn away people who might just be able to add to our knowledge and understanding?

In the middle of this are eight staff attempting to do a job of work with 20 pupils. These 20 pupils go home at 3.20pm to their families, some of whom have little or no support networks. None of the 20 pupils has residential respite care. None of the 20 pupils has a caregiver who takes the child out, thus giving the family a break for a couple of hours. There is no telephone helpline in Sheffield although there is an excellent local autistic society. Yet, in the words of Elizabeth Newson: 'Autism is perhaps the most bewildering of all handicaps' (Hipgrave and Newson 1982). Some parents of pupils in The Resource will phone me at home at least once a week. I have had phone calls from parents on New Year's Day. Calls can be at 7.30 in the morning or 10 o'clock in the evening. They have no one else to talk to. Sometimes it is the pupil himself who needs to speak to me. At one stage, if the phone rang on a Sunday at 6pm, my whole family would shout, 'It'll be Jordan'. The pressure then shifts to my partner who has to deal with this. However, she likes it when the Christmas card from a parent acknowledges her patience and understanding, especially if it is accompanied by a bottle of wine. My eldest daughter says I am more patient with children in The Resource than I am with her – that one really cut deep.

Having been involved with families of children and teenagers with autism over a 14-year period, I am filled with wonder and respect at how parents and siblings cope. I know there are good times and they are rightly celebrated. However, the difficult times that all families go through seem to be multiplied and magnified when one person is on the spectrum. At times, the isolation that families and the individuals within the family feel must be unbearable. How some marriages survive can only be a testament to supreme love and understanding.

A pupil or student can be very successful in his education (academic and social) only to go home at 3.20pm and cause absolute havoc. This fact underlines the need for daily communication between home and school. It is never acceptable for parents to be having difficulties at home, even if things are fine at school. When there were only a few pupils in The Resource, I sometimes went home and thought that we had experienced a perfect day. Now there are 20 pupils, plus a few 'extras', those days do not exist any more. There is usually some crisis to attend to or a difficulty that needs addressing. Nothing is ever perfect, and so the pressure becomes tied up with an ability to turn off at the end of the day, an ability I have yet to perfect. Autism does not end at 3.20pm each day. What seems to me like a good day for a pupil could have been one fraught with tension and anxiety into which I have had little or no insight.

The teenage years for anyone can bring upheaval and pressure. Few generalisations are possible. The more I learn about people with autism or Asperger's syndrome, the more I realise that they are more individual than 'regular' people. However, if there were some way to bypass the teenage years and move straight into adulthood, I would take it for some people with ASD. For some teenagers with Asperger's syndrome, this leap straight into the world of adults would be beneficial. Back in the real world, some of our pupils test our understanding, patience and time to the limit.

DJ is a bright pupil with higher level autism (whatever that means). If we are successful together, he should obtain five GCSEs at the higher grades of A to C. The difficulty arises from the simple fact that DJ sees no intrinsic value in working for something called five A to Cs. It does not interest him, especially if it means working or revising rather than pursuing his favourite activity which is drawing Japanese cartoons. Drawing Japanese animation characters, all of which he invents himself, is something DJ is superb at. He expects everyone to share this interest, but so would I if I possessed half his artistic talents. However, to access the course at college that he wants to do and one which we think will enhance his employment opportunities, he will require these five A to C grades. DJ will accept bribery in the form of money. (I think his mother will need to take out a bank loan when the results become known.) Revision timetables have been produced with lots of time for Japanese animation included. However, the quality and quantity of revision that DJ needs almost to guarantee success in his exams will be difficult to achieve. His success or otherwise will come down to how he feels and what frame of mind he is in on any given day of the exams. DJ does not mind if he passes or fails and he certainly has no desire to please his mother, or us. Complete days have to be written off because DJ is not focused enough to complete coursework or revision, which can be exasperating for staff.

Obsessional behaviours can be a blessing and staff always try to utilise them in any way possible within the curriculum. A person's autism has to be respected within the confines and protection of The Resource. If Bill has been through four hours of mainstream lessons and comes into The Resource looking for privacy to have 'a flap', then space and time has to be found for this. However, some obsessional interests are almost impossible to accommodate.

Terry developed an obsessional interest in another pupil in The Resource. There was little point in looking for reasons why. Terry knew this other boy's timetable and would wait for him to come out of lessons. He would use repeated greetings and enquiries about his health. If this other pupil did not respond appropriately every time, then Terry would become distraught. He would sit very close to the other pupil whenever the opportunity arose. The more staff tried to 'structure' the friendship in some way either by discussing the 'rules' or attempting to arrange some time together, the more Terry became upset. This began to have an effect on the other pupil, to the point that he did not want Terry anywhere near him. His anxiety levels grew so that he did not want to come to school. Both sets of parents were very understanding and communicated with each other about the situation.

There are few options with such a difficult kind of obsessional interest other than to 'end the friendship'. Terry was told that he could not go near this other pupil and that he could not speak to him. This was very difficult for him to achieve and put a great deal of pressure on parents and staff. The level of support that Terry received had to be increased. Dinner times that should be a time of relaxation and enjoyment became times of stress for Terry. He could not control his feelings when the other pupil was in The Resource at dinner times, so staff had to go for a walk with him. Initially, there were times when Terry could not control himself, became agitated and engineered situations so that he could see the other pupil. Terry would run at the other pupil in a high state of anxiety. After several such occasions, it was agreed with parents that we would take Terry home if this happened again. This was upsetting for staff, parents and Terry. There is no happy ending to these events. For Terry to cope with his strong feelings of friendship towards this pupil takes a great deal of effort every day. There are good times followed by 'lapses'. Staff have to take each day as it comes. Progress might be measured by the number of days in a week that Terry has managed to remain in school. If this is three days one week, the following week's target will be four. We can only hope that perhaps a new, more acceptable interest will come along for Terry and help him to move on with his life.

One measure of a good service must be how it deals with these difficult phases. In seven years we have had to concede that one pupil was incorrectly placed with us. We did our best with this pupil for a year while his obsessional behaviours spiralled out of control. Parents were given as much support as staff could muster. The effect on staff when this pupil finally had to move to a residential school in another part of the country was devastating. There was a genuine feeling of loss and guilt that maybe we could have done more.

Our pupils, because of their Statement of Special Educational Need, have an annual review meeting. We began by asking all mainstream subject teachers for brief written comments. These were put together with our own views of how a pupil was progressing into a report that parents found comprehensive and interesting. No complaints were forthcoming and, despite the time commitment, these reports were deemed to be a success for all parties. However, the local education authority produced a 20-page report for each pupil that had to be completed for annual reviews. These reports take longer to complete and say very little about the pupil's progress. For special schools with 70 or more pupils, these forms must take many days of work each year. The Resource has no administrative support. Work that might reasonably be completed by a secretary in a special school has to be carried out by the teachers and support workers in The Resource. The pressure of wasting time on useless paperwork causes more stress than any other aspect of the job. Several phone calls made to the officer responsible for this pro forma resulted in my being told that I was the only professional who had complained. I would be proud of myself if that was the case, or put up my hand and admit the mistake, but I am confident that many more phone calls similar to mine were received. Three years later, the same format for reviews is still in use. I guess they have their job to do and their role to justify.

Keeping with the general theme of mistakes, we have made our fair share. This continual pressure of making it up as we go along has meant that, on occasions, tensions have arisen between staff in the team. The strength of the team lies in the strength and character of the individuals who make it up. The Resource is not a place for shrinking violets. The nature of the work requires initiative, enthusiasm and quick thinking; nor is it a place for anyone who has a thin skin. On a good day, it is relatively easy to remember that autism is not usually personally directed. On a bad day, it can be extremely difficult not to take things personally. Maintaining a professional stance, no matter what, can be extremely stressful. The individual members of the staff team all have strong personalities and characteristics, which enable them to survive in such a fast-moving, unpredictable environment. This does mean, however, that we do not always see things the same way, which can lead to tensions within the team. These tensions have to be addressed through department meetings. However, there has also been a general acceptance that sometimes the team are just too hard on themselves. Despite the fact that it is made clear that mistakes are all right, there is tremendous pressure (and professional pride) to perfect an approach for the benefit of a pupil.

There is little hierarchy in evidence in The Resource. In practice, everyone does much the same job on a day-to-day basis, with some extra responsibility being taken by the second teacher. This has only been possible because The Resource has attracted support staff who are prepared to put in extra effort and time. Staff have high levels of skill and qualifications which set them far above the job description of child care assistants (which in Sheffield still includes watering plants and mending the dressing-up clothes). Because of this, there is some blurring of the roles between support staff and the two teachers in The Resource, which has both negative and positive implications.

The second teacher's role remains a difficult position to fill and requires a very special individual. On the one hand, s/he has to be willing and able to act as deputy for the teacher in charge, while on the other, s/he may well be treated by some mainstream teachers as a 'helping hand'. This can be the thin end of the wedge for some teachers and there is a limit to the length of time people can remain positive under such pressure.

The low pay and lack of a career progression route for support workers has meant a larger turnover of staff and a sickness record that is less than is desirable. Working so closely with pupils leaves staff vulnerable to any bugs that are circulating. Children with ASD rarely have any time off school for illness. One teacher was off sick with stress for a year before the matter was resolved with his resignation. Unfortunately, one wonderful support worker was diagnosed with cancer which led to her untimely and tragic death. Staff sickness has led to a number of cover workers being used, some good and others not. This continual change of personnel is never satisfactory for children with ASD. It has inevitably meant that the core of regular, experienced staff has had to support and sometimes carry the newer members of the team. It also contributes to the stresses and strains that other staff feel.

In a large team of eight workers, there have been times when our bonds of togetherness have been severely tested. People, however professional, sometimes bring their own personal difficulties into school. A solid team should be able to support individual colleagues who are experiencing hard times. We are a close team and try to be supportive to each other, but this is not always easy in the working environment. Then there are the days when one word, quite innocently spoken, can cause upset and anger for a colleague. Given the pressure of work that is imaginative, creative and yet based within the confines of secondary education, the staff in the team do a brilliant job.

# 4

# Counselling

The first five years in the life of the Integrated Resource represented a time of enormous growth and development on a number of levels. The Resource was developing and evolving as staff and pupil numbers increased. In line with this, the staff team recognised the need to increase their knowledge and understanding of ASD. Some of the team satisfied this need through devouring books written on every aspect of autism which they could get their hands on. As a result, together we probably have one of the best collections of books on ASD in the locality. Others felt the need for training and further relevant qualifications and sought to satisfy this through enrolling on a variety of courses. We all reflected endlessly on our practice and constantly questioned our approach. Ironically, as our knowledge and understanding of ASD increased, the more dissatisfied some of us became with that knowledge and understanding. Autism is an extremely elusive condition and it always seemed that there was more for us to learn and understand. The courses and books were all enjoyable, fascinating and informative but, with the exceptions of the autobiographical accounts such as *Emergence Labelled Autistic* (Grandin and Scarieno 1986), they never seemed quite to satisfy our need to understand. For some of us, this created a sense of inadequacy. It took us a little while to realise that this was not because we had difficulties understanding, but because we were looking to find understanding in the wrong places.

Sacks (1995) expresses the view that, despite the considerations of 'foremost writers of the day', the ultimate understanding of autism still eludes us. He considers that understanding
ASD requires a conceptual leap, which is beyond anything which
we (that is, people who do not have ASD) can dream of.
Neuro-typical people can only view ASD in a neuro-typical,
non-autistic way. We slowly began to realise that the 'conceptual
leap' which Sacks talked about required a shift of thinking on our
part and that perhaps understanding ASD required understanding 'autistic thinking'. More than that, it required us to try to
think 'autistically'.

We had always recognised the contribution which the autobiographical writings had made to our understanding of autism.
We now realised that if we were really looking to inform our
practice, then our best teachers were the people who have autism
themselves: in other words, our pupils should become our
teachers. This seems so obvious in retrospect, but at the time it
was a huge leap in our understanding and development.

One of the factors which makes ASD so fascinating and
elusive as a subject of study is that it presents itself in widely
varying individual forms. This has been described by Digby
Tantum (1999) as 'more individual than individual'. We were
confronted with this quite early on in the history of The
Resource, when we admitted our second year intake of students.

It is not an exaggeration to say that the pupils who arrived at
the Resource during the second year did more as a group to accel-
erate our understanding of ASD than perhaps any other year
group since. They presented challenges that stretched our
abilities, skills and understanding in ways in which they had not
been challenged before or since. The dynamics of the group
required that we deal with areas and issues for which, search as we
might, we were unable to find advice and guidance. Unfortunately, we wasted a considerable amount of time searching before
we realised that we were entering uncharted territory and essentially we would have to 'go it alone'. This was quite daunting,

because, as always, we were plagued with feelings of self-doubt, anxiety and inadequacy. We didn't know at the time whether we were being brave, naive or just plain silly, but we decided as a group to 'grasp the nettle'. This resulted in the development of two ASD specific teaching packages. One was a personal and social education package, which is examined elsewhere. The other is a 'counselling' package, which is now used as a tool to enable young people who have ASD to understand how the condition affects them and to help them learn how to 'manage' their own autistic behaviours.

### The background to the counselling package

Richard was one of the four pupils who formed the second-year intake of students at The Resource in 1995. He came to us from a mainstream primary school where his autistic needs and behaviours had not been recognised and, as a result, not met. Credit for enabling him to survive this experience must go to his parents who were very skilled in supporting him, both academically and socially. At first, Simon appeared to be a bundle of anxiety and self-consciousness. During his last year in primary school he had received some support for his 'learning difficulties', but this was not ASD specific. As a result, he had felt greatly misunderstood and his confidence was at an all-time low. I was appointed to work one-to-one with him during his first year at The Resource. He was fully supported in all lessons for the first term, the main target being to improve his confidence level, which would then enable more ASD specific targets to be set for him.

As Richard's academic achievement improved, so did his confidence, and we began to see different behaviours and character traits emerge. He was an intelligent boy, who had a high level of awareness of his difficulties, and also a great ability to manage and control some of them. One of his great loves in life was an area which appeared to be beyond anyone's control – teasing. He would happily tease anyone and everyone, all day and every day. He was extremely skilled at this, and had developed subtle teasing techniques which were only evident if staff employed extreme vigilance. He also had an uncanny knack of identifying everyone's Achilles heel, and would focus on this to the exclusion of all else. This was obviously very enjoyable and stimulating for him, but became increasingly wearing and challenging for any-one who was working closely with him: in this instance, me. He stretched my patience and skills to their absolute limit, and there were times when only my professional role and my personal quest to find solutions enabled me to distance myself from what was an extremely difficult and frustrating situation. The real problems occurred, however, when Richard focused his teasing on other pupils, particularly those who were in mainstream.

All the pupils in Richard's tutor group had been made aware of the nature of the difficulties experienced by the two Resource pupils who were in their class, through a specific time slot in their tutorial period. As a group of 11- and 12-year-olds, they were unbelievably understanding and supportive. As well as having two pupils with ASD in their class, they had to cope with two extra adults 'shadowing' them throughout the day, not only in lesson time but also during what would normally have been unsu-pervised time. Gaining the trust and acceptance of this group was therefore essential for the support staff to work effectively. (This has been the case with all the groups where we have been involved supporting students.) Mutual trust and acceptance is a prerequisite for the individual progress and development of all the Resource pupils. This is particularly the case for the develop-ment of independence skills, which requires a high level of trust on both sides. It is consequently an area which requires a high level of skill from the staff in The Resource.

At the time, I had two daughters aged 10 and 14 and I thought that I was relatively 'in touch' with this age group. I quickly dis-covered that I had a lot to learn. Gaining their trust and accep-tance meant that my senses had to be very selective or, more ap-propriately, 'de-selective' in what they picked up on. When support is at its most effective, mainstream students forget that there is an adult in the room with them. It is on these occasions that one requires the most selectivity, particularly in terms of what is overheard. However, in these situations one may also need to intervene, while avoiding being considered a 'spy in the camp', or compromising one's own professional position. This is a very thin line that all support staff have to tread and requires great sensitivity and tact. We do not always get it right, but experience had taught us that pupils prefer us to err on the side of caution. At the end of the day they do recognise that we have professional and adult responsibilities and are usually grateful for this.

Gaining the trust and acceptance of mainstream pupils is an ongoing task, year on year. It means that there are always battles to be won on many fronts. One of the main ones is to dispel the myth that Resource pupils have extra privileges. It is on this front that we are most often challenged by mainstream pupils. Staff who work with pupils who have ASD understand and tolerate behaviours which are not deemed acceptable in most mainstream schools. This is extremely difficult for mainstream pupils to understand, but is particularly difficult for those pupils who exhibit similar behaviours themselves. Every secondary school has pupils who feel misplaced and misunderstood by the education system. Schools approach the management of these young people differently, but it is probably fair to say that these pupils often find that their behaviour is not met with the same approach and understanding as the pupils who have ASD. They understandably find this unfair and unjust and often react aggressively. We find, however, that it is precisely this group of young people whom we have to 'win over' in order for the Resource pupils to gain any of the independence necessary for their social development and full integration. Our experience has also taught us that, once on our side, this group of young people is our biggest ally. They can always be relied on to 'look out for', befriend and defend Resource pupils if ever the need arises.

Over the years, we have found that there are two important factors in winning the trust and acceptance of mainstream pupils on behalf of Resource staff and pupils:

1.  We must show all pupils the same respect and understanding, based on their individual needs, as we show to Resource pupils.

2.  Justice must be seen to be done!

This has meant that school rules and sanctions must be seen to apply to Resource pupils. Where this is not appropriate, other visible methods of sanctions have to be employed. Richard's tutor group contained some 'rough diamonds', most of whom were extremely supportive and understanding of his difficulties. However, his teasing, which was not only directed at Resource staff and pupils, pushed them further than they could be reasonably expected to cope with. In fact, Richard's teasing was now presenting a very real barrier to his further development and acceptance within his peer group.

Around this time, Richard was also asking questions about other people's difficulties. I had told him that my daughter had dyslexia and he found this fascinating and wanted to understand it better. He was acutely aware of his own learning difficulties and was frustrated by them, and was also asking why other pupils were in The Resource and what their difficulties were. Like many young people in Sheffield who had ASD at that time, Richard had not been given a clear diagnosis of ASD. The preferred term, severe communication disorder, was used. On reflection, this was not helpful and I think probably prevented many young people and their parents from receiving appropriate help and support.

The term autism is now used quite freely in The Resource and many pupils, some of whom have ASD and some who don't, will openly ask questions about the condition. In the first two years of development of The Resource, this was not the case, however. I believe that this was directly linked to the LEA's reluctance to use the term autism and the knock-on effect this had on staff's perceptions and awareness. As a consequence, when Richard was asking questions about his own difficulties, we felt ill equipped to answer. The staff team were convinced that Richard showed autistic traits and thought that he probably had an autistic spectrum disorder, but at that time lacked the confidence and expertise in what is a very specialised area. We also felt that Richard was showing us clearly that he was aware that he was 'different' and that he needed to understand his differences and the difficulties he was experiencing. When we talked to his parents about this, it was clear that they, like many parents in the same situation, were also in need of a more helpful assessment and diagnosis. The labelling of disorders has a history of being controversial and there will always be people who argue in favour of not using labels. The staff at The Resource, together with Richard's parents, took the view that an accurate assessment and understanding of Richard's condition was needed in order to help him manage his difficulties, which he was clearly showing us he needed to do. In order to do this, an accurate and specific diagnosis was required. Initially we felt that the area of diagnosis was out of our hands, but decided to try to challenge it anyway. Little did we know at the time that this was the beginning of a journey into what was hugely uncharted territory. This is the area which, for want of a better term, we called 'counselling' young people about autism.

Altering Richard's Statement of Special Educational Needs to include the term 'autism' was the easiest part of this process as all that was required was an updated full psychological assessment. When this was achieved, we somewhat naively thought this would be the end of our role in this process. How wrong we were. This proved to be only the beginning.

Counselling is now a well-recognised and respected profession in its own right. Its contribution to other professions such as medicine and social work is acknowledged. We realised that in counselling young people who had autism we were working in two extremely specialised fields, but didn't for a moment doubt that the expertise to advise us and to 'counsel' Richard would be available somewhere. We had no idea at the time that this would lead us on a search which would prove futile and would result in us taking a huge leap into what was for us 'the unknown'.

We began with phone calls and letters to obvious academics, professionals and societies in Britain, some of whom were based in Sheffield. Some replied and some didn't. All but one were unable to offer any help. Fred Parsons, from Whitegates Adult Services in Worksop proved to be our saviour. He visited us as a team, confronted our preconceptions and challenged our way of thinking, which gave us confidence to move forward. In particular, Fred challenged our approach to answering Richard's questions and helped us recognise that presenting autism to him in the context of 'many people have difficulties' was shying away from the issues of autism and what that meant on an individual level for him. He pointed out to us that the messages we had been giving Richard were that he was 'the same as everyone else', when he already knew that this was not the case. What he really needed to understand was the ways in which he was 'different'.

Fred also gave us a loose framework for 'counselling', using Wing's Triad of Impairment. This provided the core base of a six-week counselling programme for Richard. Since then, it has been developed and expanded for use with many more students, providing a strategy which can be adopted by other professionals in similar situations to ours.

All the staff at The Resource view counselling pupils about their autism as a very special and often essential aspect of the work. It requires a great deal of skill and sensitivity, as well as considerable theoretical knowledge. It is not an automatic procedure for all of the pupils in The Resource, nor is there a prescribed time or age for commencing it. It is essentially pupil-led, in terms of the pupils indicating their desire to understand, its timing and appropriateness. Its success is difficult to measure and pupils' reactions are very individual. In almost all instances where we have 'counselled' pupils, the initial response has been mainly anger. This has been in the form of 'Why didn't someone tell me this before?' Sometimes students have difficulties coming to terms with the fact that they have a disability and this has triggered a temporary return to more severe autistic behaviours. As the sessions progress, however, pupils discover that they do not have to be disabled by their disability, and that there are many positive aspects of having an autistic spectrum disorder. Some pupils, once they understand ASD, have tried to use it as an excuse for increasing their inappropriate behaviours. The Resource staff are aware that this might happen, and on the occasions when it has this has been managed within the counselling framework. It has never lasted for any length of time. We do not always manage to 'reach' our pupils this way. There have been some instances when the timing has not been right, or it has not been thought appropriate for a variety of reasons to progress further than one or two sessions. Sometimes a break is needed. On one occasion, we considered that it was necessary to revisit the whole pro-gramme later in the year. We try to be guided by our pupils wherever possible, and their indications so far suggest that coun-selling is effective, enjoyable and ultimately helpful.

## The counselling programme

Essentially, the counselling sessions are seen as fun. The pupil is very involved in identifying a suitable time, place and name for them. On occasions, the pupil has chosen the member of staff who is to be his 'counsellor'. The staff team are not unanimously agreed about the correctness of this, as we recognise that staff have different areas of strength and pupils may choose staff for reasons other than their counselling skills. The member of staff's relationship with that pupil and his parents must also be a major factor of consideration. In practice, this is always under negotia-tion. We are still learning, and our practice is continuously evolving. The big attraction for the pupil is that the session time is found by withdrawing them from one mainstream lesson a week, and the pupil is involved in choosing this lesson. Curiously, there is rarely any conflict over this. Our pupils recognise where their strengths lie and in practice, if given the choice, will choose the lesson which is least 'autism friendly'. This is usually the same one that staff would independently choose. Over the years, the mainstream subject teachers at the school have come to understand the nature of autism. As a result, they do not take personal offence if their subject is chosen more than once.

The first 'counselling package', inspired by Richard's need to understand his difficulties, consisted of six weekly sessions which Richard chose to name 'personal time'. These took place in one of The Resource classrooms, with the teacher in charge. It centred primarily on autism as it related to Richard. Through use with other pupils, it has been modified, extended and individualised to provide a strategy which can be adapted to fit the needs of most of the pupils in The Resource who have ASD.

The staff at The Resource recognise that counselling is an extremely skilled and sensitive area, which ideally ought to be carried out by trained counsellors. For our pupils, this requires the dual skills of autism specific counselling. Our search for this, in 1995, proved futile and we reluctantly felt that we had no alternative but to 'do it ourselves'. We do not want to devalue counselling by giving the impression that anyone can do it, or that we counsel all our students as a matter of course. To date, we have counselled six of our pupils. We have found on each occasion that our effectiveness depends on our level of skills and preparation. Not all staff in The Resource want to be involved in this area. Those who do take it very seriously and recognise that a high level of research, study and preparation is needed before we begin. As this is in addition to the normal support duties, this has to be in private time. As our counselling skills have developed, so has our counselling package and our expectations of staff. We now have guidelines for staff who wish to undertake counselling, some of which are included below.

**Guidelines**

Staff should not consider embarking on this programme without first of all ensuring the following:

1. A careful and accurate assessment has been made to ensure the 'need appropriateness' for the programme. This must involve parents and other professionals working with the young person.

2. Parents' confidence and support has been won, as well as their permission and desire to participate.

3. There exists a well-established, secure but professional relationship with the young person.

4. Professional practice is grounded in theory and experience of autism and personal skills are in place for this type of one-to-one teaching. This includes personal study in the following areas:

   - *communication*, specifically:

     – all areas of non-verbal communication

     – social skills

     – use of language

   - *autism*, specifically:

     – Wing's Triad of Impairment

     – theory of mind

     – recommended teaching methods

   - *the self*, specifically:

     – development of the self concept

     – self-awareness.

     – self-esteem

     – personality development

   - *counselling*, specifically:

– methods and approaches

– practical skills

Practical tips are also given to assist staff in the delivery of the programme as follows:

1.  People who have autism cannot be relied on to 'pick things up'. Be explicit, unambiguous and specific.

2.  People who have autism often take language literally, so the use of metaphors and figures of speech should be avoided.

3.  People with autism are visual learners, so utilise it in your methods.

4.  People who have autism may not understand abstract concepts such as the 'self' or 'time'. Always check, to ensure understanding.

**The approach**

The staff at The Resource have always recognised the individuality of people who have autism, and all our reading in preparation for 'counselling' reflects and emphasises this. Our approach is not, as a result, prescriptive. We do make suggestions which ensure that the programme is autism specific in terms of its structure, content and delivery. We recommend that initially the programme follows a set period of time, which the pupil is made aware of, and incorporates the following structures:

1.  It should take the form of a one-to-one lesson in a specified classroom in The Resource with a set time, which is timetabled. In practice, this is a one-hour slot which has free time built into it. The actual counselling session usually lasts for about 40 minutes.

2.  The session must be viewed positively by all parties concerned and the pupil should be involved in naming the lesson.

3.  Sessions must be carefully planned and suitable resources thoughtfully considered and provided. In practice, we make suggestions for reading and resources, in all the relevant areas.

4.  Session evaluations should be used to direct and inform future planning.

5.  The sessions must be structured, but also need to be flexible enough to accommodate the unexpected. If this happens, it is important that we do not lose control.

At the end of the specified period, we assess whether to continue to develop the programme further. In practice, we have found that once the process has begun it continues after the set period, but without its formal structure.

### The counselling programme

The programme has evolved through use and has been designed to be flexible. It provides a framework for staff to work within, with strategies for delivering the different areas, which they may or may not use, depending on the need, appropriateness and interests of the pupil. Staff are encouraged not to make any assumptions about pupils, as our experience has taught us that these are very often wrong. Because of this, we must carefully assess each pupil's knowledge, awareness and skills in all areas of the programme, before starting, in order to determine the usefulness of the suggestions given. There are essentially three parts to the 'counselling' programme, covering the following topics:

- *Part 1* covers: knowledge of the self

- *Part 2* covers: knowledge and understanding of autism.

- *Part 3* covers: the personal management of autism.

Each part of the programme has suggested aims, which may or may not be suitable for each individual pupil. Again, these are not prescriptive, but suggestions which help the 'counsellor' to focus on suitable aims for the particular student with whom they are working. New aims can be written if those suggested are not appropriate. Similarly, Part 1 of the programme could be omitted if considered unnecessary for a particular pupil. Some examples of the suggested aims for the programme are shown at the end of this chapter.

As autism is so very individual, we very much encourage an individual approach within the overall framework. In this way, pupils' interests can be utilised. To accommodate this, the sessions are delivered in a variety of ways: e.g. games; different types of art work; writing; watching videos; social cartoons or discussions. Some examples of these are also included at the end of this chapter.

At The Resource, we have always worked closely with the parents of our pupils, communicating on a daily basis with them by dictaphone. Because of this, we view our work very much as a partnership with parents, and this is a fundamental part of our approach to counselling. Parents of our pupils are involved at the very beginning of the process in identifying and approving of the appropriateness of counselling for their child. Their consent is sought and given before the programme commences. In practice, we have found that parents have already been considering the best way to increase their child's understanding of autism before we suggest it. When they give their consent, they want to be active participants in the process and usually welcome the involvement. This means that homework is given, which develops and extends the work covered in the session. It also ensures that parents are fully informed and involved at every stage of the counselling. As a result, we minimise potential difficulties in what could be a very vulnerable time for everyone concerned. Again, examples of the type of homework set are given at the end of the chapter.

Autism is presented in a positive way throughout all sessions and is celebrated as something special. This is particularly important in the second part of the programme, which looks at autism as a disability. This is shocking news for most of our pupils, who have recognised that everyone else is out of step with them, but have never seen themselves as out of step. We use the Triad of Impairment to help focus and direct our sessions, and to provide a visual image of autism with which our pupils can identify on a personal level. We balance this against what can be termed 'the enhancements of autism', emphasising that with every difficulty there is a compensatory strength. We take the view that autism is a disability, but that it doesn't have to be disabling. For some pupils like DJ, who have no difficulties with the concept of self, this may be where they begin the programme. It is not easy for them, or the counsellor, as coming to terms with having a disability is difficult for anyone. It is doubly difficult when that disability is as subtle and invisible as autism and more particularly Asperger's syndrome. For DJ, it was the most painful and shocking revelation he could have received. He informed us loudly and angrily that 'I'm not disabled!' From there, he went on to become the biggest advocate for counselling imaginable. He is often seen and heard explaining the intricacies of autism to other Resource and mainstream pupils and has even made a video of himself, describing his counselling experience. The rest of this chapter looks at the counselling package, through the experience of DJ, otherwise known as Dominic.

Dominic came to The Resource from a mainstream primary school in September 1996. He is an extremely intelligent young man who has 'high functioning autism'. When you first meet Dominic, his intellectual ability is immediately apparent. When he first came to The Resource, he did not understand that other people, particularly other 11-year-olds, did not value his knowledge and opinions. Dominic is also outspoken and he had no awareness of speaking out of turn. He had (and still has) a very loud voice, which he would use unpredictably in lessons, sometimes to correct the class teacher. Usually his comment was correct, but it was rarely appreciated. His thought processes would often sidetrack and he would contribute to class discussions in a way which to the teacher and mainstream pupils seemed 'bizarre' or rude. Dominic has a terrific sense of humour, which is extremely individualistic and very 'autistic'. This was not always appreciated, particularly in the middle of a lesson such as history. His behaviour was very unpredictable, which made it difficult for his support teacher to anticipate situations and attempt to defuse them, or to redirect him. He was greatly misunderstood by his peer group and many of the mainstream staff. His mother says that 'people either love him or hate him' and I think that this is very true.

When Dominic started at secondary school, his peer group had never met anyone quite like him and they hated him. At the beginning of Dominic's first year this was manageable because he was fully supported in all lessons and consequently protected from difficult situations. As Dominic's independence level increased, however, so did the problems. By the beginning of Year 8, these problems were of an almost unmanageable proportion. If left independent, even for short periods of time, Dominic became the subject of physical bullying, which very quickly accelerated to a potentially dangerous situation for him. This initiated increased tutorial work with his peer group, but it also initiated counselling for Dominic to enable him to understand why people found his behaviour unacceptable, and also to enable him to manage his autistic behaviours.

I see Dominic as a very special young man and consider myself extremely privileged to have been the person who counselled him about his autism. It was one of the most challenging and rewarding experiences of my working life. Dominic helps to bridge the gap between neuro-typical and autistic thinking. Because of this, he has taught us such a lot as a Resource team. We belong to the group of people who love him.

Dominic was already familiar with the word 'autism, as it had been used freely at home. He was aware that this was something, which he 'had' and he saw it as something which made life difficult for him and got him into fights. He felt very misunderstood and confused and wanted to understand why people didn't like him. He was very willing to have special lessons to help him to understand, especially when he discovered that the time for them would be found by withdrawing him from his hated history lesson. I think that his title for these lessons, 'tacky autism lessons' – abbreviated to TAL, demonstrates both his feelings for the condition and his sense of humour. It was initially intended that four to six lessons would be required to cover what was at that stage a basic 'autism awareness' package. This was extended to ten formal sessions, which Dominic chose to continue on a less formal basis afterwards.

The first part of the programme aimed to increase Dominic's understanding of autism as a disability, while viewing it as a positive aspect of him. This involved presenting it as something which made him special, and also explaining to him the nature of autism as a spectrum disorder which is distinct from intelligence. This may sound academic and theoretical, but no one who has ever worked with Dominic has doubted his ability to grasp difficult concepts if they are explained to him in a suitable way. On this occasion, that proved to be right.

I began the first session in fear and trepidation. On occasions like this, one expects the unexpected and that is sometimes a very daunting position in which to be. However, I had prepared thoroughly and felt relatively confident that I knew Dominic well enough to cope with whatever he threw at me; still, one never knows.

The first part of the session was relatively easy. Dominic is very articulate, so it began with a general discussion about disability. We looked at pictures of people, some of whom had physical disabilities, and some who had hidden disabilities such as deafness, dyslexia and autism. Dominic talked about a girl on the school minibus who was profoundly deaf. He recognised that she had a disability, but was very angry that autism was being classed as a disability. He shouted at me (which he used to do quite often then) 'Do you mean I have a disability?' I will always remember the quizzical look he gave me when I replied, 'Yes, but it doesn't mean that you're disabled.' Often, events in The Resource are quite unpredictable. We have to 'think on our feet' and frequently we rely on intuition, combined with knowledge gained from our reading, to guide our actions. Sometimes this makes us feel that we are making things up as we go along. Sometimes we are. Often we feel quite isolated and alone, which can be frightening as we are all very aware of the possible effects of misguided actions. This was one occasion when I felt all of these things at once. I was committed to seeing this through, however, so I suggested that we look at the pictures again. Dominic calmly started going through them.

This time, we selected three pictures, including one of the person who had autism and an athlete in a wheelchair, and made two lists. One list was of the difficulties that people with this type of disability experienced and the other was of things they were unable to do because of it. We looked at the things that Dominic found difficult and he identified understanding other people and getting into fights all the time. In this context, Dominic found it easy to recognise the difference between having a disability and being disabled, arguing that, for example, there was nothing a blind person couldn't do, providing they had the right help and equipment, except see. He then said, 'From now on, the only fight that I'm going to have is with autism.'

The second part of the session looked at autism as a spectrum disorder. Dominic has always been good at science subjects and he had recently been studying light in his physics lessons. Because of this, the idea of a spectrum was not new to him. We used a drawing of a rainbow to represent the autistic spectrum, with classic autism at one end and Asperger's syndrome at the other. Once this had been explained to Dominic, he immediately started talking about other people he knew, placing them at various points on the rainbow. When asked to place himself somewhere on the rainbow, he chose just below Asperger's syndrome. Many of us are still confused by the distinction between Asperger's syndrome and 'high functioning autism'. For some reason, Dominic seemed clear on this. In *Autism: An Inside-Out Approach* Donna Williams (1996) states that: 'Most high functioning people with autism or Asperger Syndrome can tell who has what and we gravitate in the direction of those who most share our own system, provided the level of functioning is similar.' Perhaps this is why Dominic had such clarity.

Dominic was quite fascinated by the work we were doing and was really keen to begin every session. Homework was a regular feature of the sessions, which we would discuss at the beginning of the following week. This in itself presented a major break-through, as Dominic had always been reluctant to do homework, seeing it as a contradiction in terms. The Triad of Impairment fascinated him and he loved its visual nature. We looked at the three areas of the Triad, first identifying Dominic's strengths and then his difficulties in each area. This was a revelation to him. He began to see some of his difficulties in a new light, and was very proud of the 'special' areas which we identified. He refused point blank to accept that he might have any imagination difficulties and was particularly proud of his strengths in this area. Dominic has always had a superb memory and wrote brilliant, witty, but 'bizarre' stories. He also had a very 'wacky' sense of humour and an obsession with drawing cartoon characters, which took on a Japanese animation style. At the time, I viewed these as very positive compensations for what I saw as his imagination difficulties. I put these to Dominic and he accepted most of them. He had no difficulty accepting that like most people who have autism, he is very rigid. He also had no difficulty in accepting that he was unable to empathise with people, and could not see that anyone else had a different point of view. He found my views on his rigid style of drawing difficult to accept, however. Then he said, 'Do you mean… like …I have difficulty drawing from real life?' I said that was exactly what I meant. He thought about it for a little while and then said, 'I wish I could draw from real life… then I could draw dogs playing poker!' Dominic also had what everyone thought of as an imaginary friend called Amy, whom he took everywhere with him. This was one area of difficulty that he refused to accept and I judged it better not to pursue it. Three years later, in a mainstream lesson discussion, Dominic told his classmates how he was angry with his mother because when he was seven he had met a beautiful little girl in a playground. He had been taken away from her in order to go home and had never seen her again. This little girl was called Amy. It was no wonder that he would not accept everyone else's view that she was imaginary.

The more we have worked with people with autism, the more they challenge our conventional, neuro-typical viewpoint. I now have difficulty with the view of the Triad, which presents a rather negative view of autism and views people like Dominic as having an imagination 'impairment'. Dominic has a brilliant imagination. It's not like mine and it may not be like yours, but it is brilliant and unique. When seen this way, how can it be an impairment?

Despite this, the Triad of Impairment continues to provide a useful visual image, which in this instance helped Dominic to focus on the strengths and difficulties which he had and was experiencing with his classmates. It also offered him a way in, through which he was able to deal with them. He was quite taken with it and immediately started applying it to other people. Interestingly, he identified Homer Simpson as having autism. Since then, I watch the Simpsons in quite a new light.

One of the most difficult moments for me was when Dominic asked me if he could 'take that triangle thing home to work on with my dad'. It transpired that he was quite convinced that his father had autism and felt he would benefit from 'that triangle thing'. I had such mixed emotions. I was thrilled that Dominic felt that because he found the Triad useful, then someone else would; I was also quite delighted that he was able to identify autistic traits in someone else, albeit his father. For a short while, I didn't know what to do. Dominic was so positive about its usefulness and appropriateness that in the end I didn't have the heart to say no. It is at times like these that our partnership with the parents of our pupils is really tested. Dominic went home with a cardboard drawing of the Triad of Impairment in his bag and a dictaphone message to his mother from me, explaining the situation. She told me later that the cardboard drawing was used and that Dominic's father does now acknowledge that he has autistic tendencies.

Once Dominic understood the Triad of Impairment, he went from strength to strength. He talked about 'beating autism', which I was quite uncomfortable with. I see autism as being very much a part of Dominic, and it seemed to me that he was denying a part of himself. I had tried so hard to present autism in a positive way and began to feel I had failed him in some way. Dominic uses very strong words to explain his feelings and as time has gone on I have realised that he was just expressing his frustration. He has a very positive view of autism, but recognises that there are aspects of it which the rest of us find difficult. This is very frustrating for him. Over the years in The Resource, we have learnt that if we follow our pupils' lead, then they push the boundaries in ways which we would never have anticipated. So I decided to 'go with him', which resulted in a very individualistic approach to the next part of the counselling programme – 'Managing Autism'.

The aims of this part of the counselling were to identify those situations which Dominic found difficult to cope with. Once identified, they were to be prioritised by Dominic and we would then work on strategies which would help him to manage the situation better. I also wanted to encourage Dominic to feel in control of them. Dominic had no difficulty in providing a list of situations which were difficult for him, nor did he have difficulty prioritising them. At the top of his list, and the area which he wanted to work on most, was 'not getting on with teachers'. At the time I was surprised that teachers took priority over his peer group. In retrospect, I see the importance for Dominic.

We worked on each item on Dominic's list, breaking them down and providing strategies, based on Dominic's strengths, which would help him to manage what in effect was someone else's behaviour. An example of this was that Dominic learnt to identify which teachers he could make jokes with and those with whom it was better not to. He also learnt that some teachers interpreted his answering back to them as 'rude' and would get angry. He impressed us all (and still does) with his ability to put this into practice in lessons. Once the process had begun and different strategies were identified, Dominic quickly worked through the whole list. We had decided at the beginning of this stage that we would have a visual means of disposing of the difficulties, once Dominic had learnt to manage them. For some reason, Dominic decided that they should be 'exterminated'. It would have been great to set fire to them, but I didn't think this would be considered appropriate in school. Instead, we had a small 'extermination bin', where each individual area of difficulty was put and disposed of once it no longer presented as a difficulty.

I still have problems with this, and can get quite annoyed at the inability of mainstream society to understand and accommodate people who are outside societal norms. I often question the logic which dictates that people with autism have to manage and control their behaviours and responses to an extent which sometimes causes extreme stress, and even on some occasions mental illness. There will always be a dilemma for me in this. I understand that for many people who have autism, the only way they can function within mainstream society is by conforming to the norms and expected behaviours, but it still doesn't sit comfortably with me. Dominic, like many other people who have autism, doesn't seem to have too many difficulties with this.

### Dominic's Comments

As I said earlier, Dominic has become a great advocate of counselling to the point where he made a video, which has been since used as a teaching tool on many courses on autism. The following comments from the video are his.

Before I knew about the disability of autism, I wasn't really aware of much at all. I did wonder why I acted a bit stupid sometimes, but I wasn't really thinking much about it. Perhaps people didn't tell me because they thought I wouldn't understand. I also have diabetes so life can be a bummer sometimes.

I thought, why is autism a communication disorder, if it affects how I behave not how I speak? Before I knew about autism, teachers were like enemies to me. They threw hard work at me like it was hell or something.

When I was first told the name of my disability, I thought 'What the hell is that?' I was confused and angry, as usual. I thought, 'This would have to happen to me, wouldn't it?' I began to realise why people in The Resource behaved a bit differently. Before I knew, I didn't really understand other people, and they didn't really understand me. Very often, because of this misunderstanding, I got into arguments and fights.

There are some good bits about my autism. I get to skip some lessons, especially history, which is really boring. I get to come to this school because it has a special place for people like me. At The Resource, there are people who like and understand me, or at least they try. I finally have people I can rely on. I guess I may have given up on life, because nobody understood me.

Because of my autism, I've got an excuse for the dumb mistakes I might make. Mr Matthew disagrees with this reason, but he's not autistic, is he?

Life can still be tough sometimes, especially when I look ahead. Getting a job will be difficult, because not many people understand about my disability. Sometimes I get worried, even in the subjects I am supposed to be good at, e.g. maths. This may be because like most teenagers, *I hate maths.*

Getting a girlfriend has always been a problem for me. I just don't try any more. Trying's the first step towards failure. At least I know I can talk about it in The Resource.

It will be harder getting qualifications for my dream job: designing games for Playstation. I'll need at least C grades in my GCSEs, especially IT.

There is stuff that is becoming easier now I know about autism. Controlling myself is a cinch, but I might go crazy in a disco, and call it dancing! Spotting my mistakes is also getting easier. I realise now that I am not always right, in fact hardly ever (just kidding). I seem to be better at understanding other people, and in turn, they seem to be more friendly towards me.

From now on hopefully, the only fight I am going to have is with autism.

**DJ Morris, aged 13**

### Suggestions from the counselling programme

We would like to emphasise that these are only suggestions. Aims must always be based on assessment of the needs of the individual pupil.

*Aims for Part 1: knowledge of the self*

1.  To identify/establish the concept of the 'self' as distinct from others.

2.  To identify/establish the concept of the past 'self', i.e. as a baby.

3.  To identify personal character traits.

4.  To introduce the idea of 'specialness' or 'uniqueness'.

*Aims for Part 2: knowledge and understanding of autism*

1. To establish understanding of the term 'disability'

2. To create awareness of autism as a disability.

3. To foster/reinforce the idea of being 'special'.

4. To recognise and understand the terms, autism and Asperger's syndrome (may not appropriate for all students).

5. To explain autism as a communication disorder.

6. To identify what autism means specifically for [name].

7. To increase understanding of autism as a spectrum disorder which is distinct from intelligence.

*Aims for Part 3: the personal management of autism*

1. To identify situations which are difficult for the student because s/he has autism.

2. To prioritise with the student his or her main areas of difficulty.

3. To provide practical coping strategies for the student in difficult situations.

4. To encourage the student in the belief that s/he is in control of his or her autism.

5. To provide an effective strategy for minimising situations which are difficult for the student.

Games always work well with our pupils. They don't appear to be work in the formal sense of the word, but provide excellent opportunities for practising social interaction skills. They are also visual. Because of this, a carefully thought-out game can be a much more effective means of delivering a 'message' than any language based one. The following are examples of some games which we might use to deliver the first part of the programme on the self.

1.  Pupils are fascinated by the concept that adults (especially teachers) used to be babies and love this game. It provokes a great deal of discussion about time and the past. It is quite easy to build up a collection of photographs of staff as adults and babies and to ask the parents of our pupils for similar photographs of family members, including some of the pupils themselves. The game is simply for the pupil to try to match the adult with the baby. Matching them up provokes a great deal of discussion and provides many opportunities for teaching. After the pupil has learnt which baby matches which adult, you can then turn them all upside down and play the memory pairs game.

2.  Prepare as many 'role cards' as you can think of using words and pictures, ensuring that there is a high proportion which are applicable to the pupil and yourself. Examples would be: boy, woman, pupil, son, brother, man, teacher, wife, footballer, artist, father, sister, etc. Also include many which aren't applicable to either of you, for example, firefighter. Then play *Who am I? What am I? Snap!* As follows:

    Boy + Son = Snap!
    Pupil + Boy or Girl = Snap!
    Teacher + Man or Woman = Snap!
    Mother + Woman = Snap!
    Boy + Artist = Snap!

This does not have to be played quickly, as the identification of the roles will take some time and thought.

3.  A different version of this game can be used to identify different character traits. Again, prepare cards using different character traits and the names of different people on them: e.g. funny, friendly, silly, naughty, talkative, pretty. Use the pupil's name, your name, Bart Simpson's name etc. (You will probably need more than one card of you and the pupil to be most effective.) Using

these cards, play *Character Snap!* in the same way as described above. Be positive and take your time.

Friendly + Pupil = Snap!
Funny + Mr Bean = Snap!
Sporty + Pupil = Snap!

4. This game is useful for work which identifies autism as a disability. Using the pictures which you've collected of people who have disabilities and cards with a named disability on them, turn them all upside down and play the memory pairs game, to try to match the people to the disability. It is important that hidden disabilities including autism are used.

All four games provoke a great deal of discussion, which can be directed into counselling.

As people who have autism are often visual learners and thinkers, artwork is often very helpful. The following art activities may be used during different parts of the programme.

DRAWING

1. Ask the pupil to draw him or herself as a baby. Then ask them to draw themselves now. Compare the two and, if appropriate, discuss the changes.

2. Use the mirror and draw what you both think you look like then draw each other. Compare them.

MAKING

1. Make a poster by writing the character traits you have identified in the session on coloured sticky labels and stick them around a mounted photograph entitled 'What I am!' Put it on the wall.

2. For work on specialness, you can make a collage by using cut-outs of famous people from magazines and pictures of people with disabilities to make a 'They're special because…' board.

3.  Use a photo of the pupil to make an 'I'm special' poster using sticky labels as before.

4.  For work on Part 2, you can draw a large triangle on card and label it to represent the Triad of Impairment. Use simple terminology like 'getting on with people' for social interaction, etc. Using the card and two different coloured sticky labels, identify the pupil's strengths and difficulties. Write these on labels and stick them at the appropriate place on the Triad. You will have to prepare well for this in order to know the pupil's strengths and difficulties, and to which area of the Triad they belong. You can then positively guide and prompt the pupil.

5.  Alternatively, you can get the student to design a poster entitled 'Autism is special because'. Include on it facts such as 'Not many people have it' and personal details like 'It helps me to remember everyone's birthday' or 'It helps me to draw well'.

6.  To make a different collage, focusing on autism in a positive way, you identify and stick representations of strengths, for example, lists of birthdays, pictures of trains, cartoon drawings, etc.

Sometimes discussion is a suitable method of delivery. The following are suggestions for discussion:

1.  Using the photographs of adults and of themselves as children, talk about the things that have changed and the things that have stayed the same. Then do the same with photographs of the pupil.

2.  Using the role cards you have made for the *Snap!* game, talk about the roles. Identify which ones apply to you and the pupil.

3.  Using a mirror, encourage the student to describe him/herself.

4.  Using family photographs of yourself and the pupil, discuss whom you each resemble.

5. Talk about any experience the student has had of communicating with someone who has a different communication disorder, e.g. deafness. Look at books of British Sign Language signs. This could lead on to talking about different types of communication difficulties, e.g. dyslexia.

6. Talk about what having autism is like for other people, for example, Richard Exley, or anyone else the student knows.

Sometimes, there is no alternative to formal teaching, particularly in the section on autism. This can work very well if you employ visual methods. Most of our students enjoy watching videos. The following could all be used to highlight and talk about behaviour which may appear 'autistic'. They can also be used as spring-boards for discussions on alternative ways of behaving which can prevent difficult situations happening in Part 3:

- any of the *Mr Bean* videos
- *Fawlty Towers*
- *The Simpsons*
- NAS videos specifically on autism
- *I'm Not Stupid*
- Recordings of television programmes
- *Rainman*
- *Forest Gump*

*Rainman* presents an extremely stereotypical view of autism, but can nevertheless be useful. Similarly, *Forest Gump* can provide a positive image of disability.

Writing also has its uses. Students who have autism often like lists and rules. The following suggestions show how this can be utilised and all are good for provoking discussion:

1. Make two lists: one of disabilities which can be seen and one of disabilities which can't be seen. On the computer,

ask the pupil to make a table with these columns and
headings.

| What the disability is | What those people can do | What those people can't do |
|---|---|---|
| [e.g.] Blindness | Cook, eat, walk, run, sport, etc. | See |

2. Complete the table, using all the types of disabilities you
   and the pupil can think of. Challenge preconceptions, for
   example, blind people can't see, but they can still do
   everything else if they are given the right equipment and
   support. Include autism on the list.

3. Use social cartoons. Draw, or get the student to draw
   people in difficult situations. Involve the student in
   writing captions for them and providing alternative
   captions which could result in alternative outcomes or
   ways of managing difficult situations.

4. Some students can, with help, be the agony aunt on
   fictional problem pages. The problems can be made
   specific to that student.

5. Alternatively, hypothetical scenarios can be used, where
   the student writes what s/he thinks will happen.

6. Role plays or puppets can provide alternative ways for
   dealing with difficult situations.

7. Many of the above activities, particularly the artwork,
   lend themselves well to homework. They can also be used
   to reinforce the learning that has taken place.

# 5

# The National Curriculum?
## Not Quite

There are 20 pupils in The Resource at King Ecgbert School. They each have a Statement of Special Educational Needs that relates to a severe communication disorder. One of our most recent visitors was an HM inspector who was looking into the whole area of access and inclusion. Her opinion was that the pupils we cater for are in the 'top' 50 per cent of the autistic spectrum. No apology is made for the language used, as there are no adequate or appropriate words. However, this is important to mention because some of our critics suggest that we 'cream off' the more able pupils with autism. I find this terminology much less acceptable not simply because it is untrue, but, by its very nature, autism and Asperger's syndrome are severe disabilities. No apologies are made that we only cater for half of the spectrum. Honest and true attempts at inclusion and access can only cater for a proportion of pupils with additional needs. Staff at The Resource take pride in the fact that we serve half of the children on the autistic spectrum. Sometimes it takes an outside person such as an inspector to make you feel good about what you do. It seems that some professionals within the field of autism are over-critical of the work of others. None has all the answers. I suppose our critics could argue that because we take the stand-point of not having all the answers, we have nothing to offer in the continuing debate about autism. We do not want to debate, although we will always listen without judgement. We want to change things so people with autism can have access to a better deal. As John Clements and Ewa Zarkowska (2000) write: 'It is our firm belief that everyday life is the real arena of change... It is the little and not so little things, done day in and day out, that make the difference.'

Another recent visitor was Richard Exley, a brilliant young man with Asperger's syndrome. He was our choice for writing the Foreword to this book. Richard spent the day with us in The Resource, talking with pupils and staff alike. He seemed to like what we were trying to do. This is all the praise we need.

In addition to the 20 pupils, staff from The Resource support two other pupils in the school who are on the spectrum but do not have a Statement of Special Educational Needs. Once a specialist provision is established, parents of children with a diagnosis of autism or Asperger's will see the school as being perhaps more understanding towards their child. This is an extra role for staff from The Resource to play, but one that is welcomed because each new person we come across with an autistic spectrum disorder teaches us all more about the disability. However, there is no denying the extra pressure that staff are under because of pupils who come into the school with an expectation of greater awareness and understanding towards the disability. The Resource has no outreach worker to support and guide other pupils with autistic spectrum disorders in Sheffield.

The range of academic ability of these 22 pupils varies from close to a severe learning difficulty to genius. Each of these children present his or her own mixture and combination of needs that require addressing. What the pupils all have in common is that following the national curriculum will never be enough for them to achieve a broad and balanced education.

Anthony, who is chronologically a Year 10 pupil but needs access to a Year 11 curriculum because he is bored in lessons, is the same pupil who cannot relate to a sizeable majority of his peers or teachers. He is easily the most gifted pupil I have ever met with a diagnosis of Asperger's syndrome. Academically, he will take seven GCSEs a year early and should go on to do well at

A-levels and university. This will mean very little in terms of his life opportunities unless he can develop a greater understanding of his own Asperger's syndrome. Unless we can develop some method of improving his organisational skills, Anthony will continue to lose more biros than Bic can manufacture. Anthony does not have a Statement. His parents transferred him to the school during his Year 8. My first involvement came when his previous secondary school invited me to talk to Anthony's peers through a life skills lesson. I was told there was little or no understanding of the difficulties Anthony faced and that he was getting continually teased and threatened.

I went off to this school thinking I would stun and amaze these young teenagers with stories about Asperger's syndrome and how difficult life was for their friend Anthony. Their understanding and empathy would be transformed in this one-hour lesson and they would all emerge as more rounded and well-balanced individuals. Instead, I spent the hour listening to how difficult they found life with someone with Asperger's syndrome. Someone had to listen to their 'gripes' and how much self-control and understanding they were already offering to this student. I owed those students that much as I realised that Anthony's mother was correct – he could not continue in this school.

Anthony rightly transferred to King Ecgbert School and now takes up a lot of my time. Fortunately, he is also getting some support from Professor Digby Tantum of Sheffield University. After Anthony got into a fight on public transport, his mother and I also had the opportunity to develop understanding and empathy levels among members of the local constabulary, which was a real bonus, and I have to say, a pleasure.

The pupil who gives everything he has got, develops a good understanding of his autism, uses good coping strategies and continues to improve his social use of language, will need something more if he is only entered for two or three GCSEs. The national curriculum cannot provide this 'something more'. It is not designed that way.

In addition to integration into work, which is discussed in Chapter 6, staff from The Resource do their utmost to ensure that each pupil achieves his or her potential at GCSE. Our hope is that later on employers will recognise the remarkable D grades for exactly what they are – remarkable. However, at its best access and inclusion has to mean much more than this. An integrated resource should represent the very best from the special and the mainstream sectors of education. Life skills and personal and social education (PSE) are two key areas for pupils with severe communication disorders.

Staff in The Resource made the mistake (yet again) of searching high and low for a good life skills package, or even bits of one that we could use. To our credit, we were quicker to realise that if we needed a good life skills package of lessons to suit the needs of our pupils, we would have to write one ourselves. This would need to include road safety, using the telephone, recognising food items and their prices in the shops, making a menu on a budget, shopping, cooking, using public transport, eating in public, knowing your own locality, opening a bank account and using a post office. The package needed to be simple to use, with good and clear criteria for evaluation. No package is ideal; they should be working documents that are added to and extended over time. In a year, if a particular lesson or series of lessons has not been used, throw them away and re-evaluate what your pupils require.

The best life skills packages should be used in real life situations. These are where we all learn best, and this is especially true for someone with autism. However, there are occasions when it might be deemed safer to begin a series of lessons from the comfort and safety of school. Role-play has its place in this but must be used with the utmost care. The language used in role-play must cover everything you want the student to learn. 'Assume no previous knowledge' is something I repeatedly tell people in training sessions. It is also something that is difficult for a non-autistic person to achieve.

A pupil of ours was ready for some lessons on catching the bus to school. I thought it safer to role-play the situation first. I planned carefully. A zero bus pass was obtained so that the pressure of money did not cause any undue anxiety. Through role play in the safety of The Resource, I became the nice bus driver, the uncommunicative bus driver and the bus driver from hell. The pupil dealt with all of these scenarios with great skill. Over several weeks, my confidence in this pupil increased to the point that real-life teaching needed to be attempted. We caught the bus together in real life with no problems. He could recognise the correct number bus and knew where to get off for school (fortunately this was a bus terminus). We practised the walk from the terminus to school looking at all the safest places to cross the road. That nervous and scary first morning arrived when the pupil left his proud mother at home as he walked to the nearby bus stop. He returned home after five minutes complaining that the bus had not stopped. His puzzled mother returned to the stop with her son, questioning him all the way. Had he put his arm out to signal the correct number bus to stop? His mother quickly realised where the problem lay. This pupil had put his arm out for the correct bus. However, the bus was the one travelling in the opposite direction on the other side of the road. I had not covered the fact that the correctly numbered bus must also be on the correct side of the road in my teaching of this pupil. I had assumed prior knowledge. Fatal mistake.

Public transport teaching can be a nightmare area of life skills. I have found myself chasing buses containing one of our pupils because they have forgotten to get off at the allotted point. Buses that have a combination of similar numbers and letters are difficult. Unfortunately, one of our main bus routes to school is numbered 97A. Get on the plain old 97 bus and you bypass school on the way out into the beautiful countryside of Derbyshire. Sean was taught to catch the 97A bus on his way back to school after work experience. When it was an hour past his correct return time, panic set in. We had staff in cars out looking for him. To this day, I still have no idea how far he walked back to school having caught the 97 bus. He must have crossed some very busy dual carriageways on his way back to school once he had realised his mistake. He only did this once and my blood pressure soon returned to near normal.

Some of the packages of lessons in our life skills folder are shown in Tables 5.1 to 5.5. They may not suit the needs of the pupils/children you might be working/living with, but they may give you some ideas.

| *Table 5.1 Answering the telephone* | |
|---|---|
| **1. Lifts receiver and holds correctly to the ear** <br><br> When phone rings, pupil is able to lift the receiver and hold to the ear with the mouthpiece in correct position. | 0 = No response/unable at this time. <br><br> 2 = Holds receiver correctly. |
| **2. Identifies self (or location or number)** <br><br> Answers phone by stating name, location or number. | 0 = No response/unable at this time. <br><br> 1 = Answers only by saying 'Hello'. <br><br> 2 = Identifies self, location or number. |
| **3. Holds a simple conversation** <br><br> Converses with the person on the phone (if appropriate). | 0 = No response/unable at this time. <br><br> 2 = Holds a simple conversation. |
| **4. Calls appropriate person to the phone** | 0 = No response/unable at this time. <br><br> 2 = Responds and calls appropriate person to the phone. |

| **5. Takes a simple message**<br>Takes a simple message and passes it on to the appropriate person. | 0 = No response/unable at this time.<br>1 = Passes message to appropriate person but gets it mixed up.<br>2 = Passes correct message on as required. |

| *Table 5.2 Using a private telephone* | |
|---|---|
| **1. Dials and obtains required number (written down)**<br>Dials the number (7 digits). | 0 = No response/unable at this time.<br>1 = 3 to 6 digits dialled correctly.<br>2 = All 7 digits dialled correctly, number obtained. |
| **2. Asks for person concerned**<br>When number is obtained, asks for the person required (unprompted). | 0 = No response/unable at this time.<br>2 = Fully able. |
| **3. Deals with the phone call**<br>The objective of the phone call is achieved. | 0 = No response/unable at this time.<br>1 = Communicates part of message/request/information.<br>2 = Deals with the phone call in a completely satisfactory way. |

| *Table 5.3 Using a payphone* | |
|---|---|
| **1. Knows and selects appropriate coins to insert**<br>Most call boxes need 10p, 20p, 50p or £1 coins (no change is given for 50p or £1). | 0 = Not aware.<br>1 = Is aware of some coins.<br>2 = Is aware of all appropriate coins<br><br>to use. |
| **2. Lifts receiver and waits for dialling tone** | 0 = Unable.<br>2 = Fully able. |

| | |
|---|---|
| **3. Inserts the right coins**<br><br>On hearing the dialling tone (or seeing a flashing 10p coin on the screen) inserts the right coin into the slot. | 0 = No response/unable at this time.<br><br>1 = Responds but tries to put coin in wrong slot, or uses wrong coin.<br><br>2 = Responds with the correct coin in the right slot. |
| **4. Inserts more money/says goodbye when money is running out**<br><br>Responds appropriately to the instructions given. | 0 = No response/unable at this time.<br><br>2 = Knows to insert more money or<br><br>to end the conversation. |
| **5. Collects any unused coins**<br>Knows to check if any coins have been returned. | 0 = No response/unable at this time.<br><br>2 = Fully able. |

This section will be taught using role play (Figures 5.4 and 5.5).

| *Table 5.4 How to obtain the emergency services* | |
|---|---|
| **Knows how to use the phone in an emergency including**<br>(a) Dials 999.<br>(b) Asks for appropriate service.<br>(c) Knows how to give appropriate information. | 0 = No response/unable at this time.<br><br>1 = Able to perform some but not all of the requirements.<br><br>2 = Able to perform all of the requirements. |

| *Table 5.5 Using the telephone directory* | |
|---|---|
| **Uses a telephone directory with some success**<br>Starts with own name and number.<br>Uses other names known to the pupil.<br>Uses names not known to the pupil. | 0 = No response/unable at this time.<br><br>1 = Able to find correct surname, but not the specific name required.<br><br>2 = Correctly locates the required name and number. |

Staff have added to these lessons to cover such things as using a phone card. Evaluation sheets using the simple scoring system and plenty of room for detailed comments/opinions are provided for each of these lessons.

Problems can always arise, especially if something taught in life skills develops into an obsession or adds fuel to the fire. Jordan had learnt how to use the telephone, and was taught how to check numbers in the directory. However, a more advanced part of the scheme of work was to learn how to phone 192 (Directory Enquiries) and find out unknown phone numbers. His already strong interest in using the phone now knew no bounds. The headteacher of his primary school telephoned to let me know that Jordan was phoning her every day and, pleasant as that was, she needed to get on with her work. Jordan, who is also very efficient at remembering addresses, then printed a list of staff home phone numbers and pinned it up in The Resource for all to see.

As with all special interests, staff do not try to prevent them unless they are harmful to the individual pupil or to others. In addition to Jordan's interest in the telephone, he also had a strong desire to write letters. Some of these letters contained issues that we needed to pick up on in lessons. However, boundaries had to be placed on use of the telephone and letter writing. Jordan is permitted one phone call to my house at the weekend if he has had a good few days at home. Letters are still written by Jordan but he brings them to staff before they can be posted. Communication between Jordan's father and me has to be regular and honest; fortunately, we get on well. Jordan's letter writing, with a great deal of staff and parental time and input, has become much more acceptable in content and style.

Within the limited amount of time pupils spend each week in The Resource, space must be found for children with autism to work out issues for themselves. We cannot deny a pupil the right to tackle an issue in his or her own way. Staying with the same pupil, Jordan developed a strong desire to learn more about the attitude of adults towards heaven. This was sparked by the innoculation all pupils were about to receive for the meningitis C infection. Jordan, like a lot of people, was not keen on the idea of a needle going into his arm. Time was spent talking to Jordan about meningitis and what a dangerous disease it is. He asked questions at home and school about meningitis and death and

---

### Jordan's view of Heaven

Heaven is a place where people go when they die. Heaven is a free place and a happiness place where you are always happy and never feel sad or worried. Heaven is like a cartoonist place but just bright white and blue. Heaven is a really nice place where you can do whatever you like although it is not a real place. I've been telling my Dad about Heaven and he says it is not a real place because if I ask him difficult questions like what it is like in Heaven, he can't answer until he goes to Heaven because he hasn't seen it before. Some people think there is a Heaven and some people don't. You have to die to get there. I think from Earth to Heaven takes one week to get there. Now, in the dark where the planets are, you don't just go straight up. If you do you'll bang into the black. So, I think you have to turn left to get to Heaven and I think there is a passageway to Heaven. Now, we go to Heaven when you have a bad disease or some massive accident like falling into a bush or tree, or a car crash. You can go to heaven by getting meningitis. You can get meningitis if you don't have an injection in your arm. If you have it, you're fine. God is in charge of Heaven. Now, God's last name is O'Mighty. His jobs are to throw down the rain, snow and sun and sometimes he brings an eclipse when there is one. If you want to go on the computer in Heaven you can. They have parties in Heaven and I could chat with God. If it's my birthday, they could have a party for me. And now I think that is about it for Heaven. It's been nice to talk about it and I think that is all I have to say about it and that is it for now. That is all from Heaven.

---

*Figure 5.1 Jordan's view of Heaven*

honest, factual answers were given. Opinions were also given freely. The injection also came not too long after a famous soap opera star was 'killed off' in a TV programme popular with Jordan. He developed a keen interest in death and what happens next. Having questioned his parents and staff in The Resource, he took to summarising his feelings through writing. One such piece of work is shown in Figure 5.1.

Jordan did three such pieces of writing on the computer about Heaven and had deep philosophical discussions about faith, morality and eternal life. Then it stopped. Something else became a more pressing need. Because time and space was made for Jordan to explore this area of life and his feelings towards it, he moved on. However, at that time his writing on Heaven became much more important than French, PE or maths.

A good PSE package is a very difficult proposition. First of all, you have to accept that you are going into yet another area that is a long way beyond the reaches of the national curriculum. Some of the areas which need to be taught are outside the law as it stands at present in this country. The first thing we decided to do, in the time-honoured tradition when one does not have any answers, was to ask someone else what they thought we should be teaching. We sent a questionnaire to all parents, the experts (Figure 5.2). A draft policy was also sent to parents (Figure 5.3).

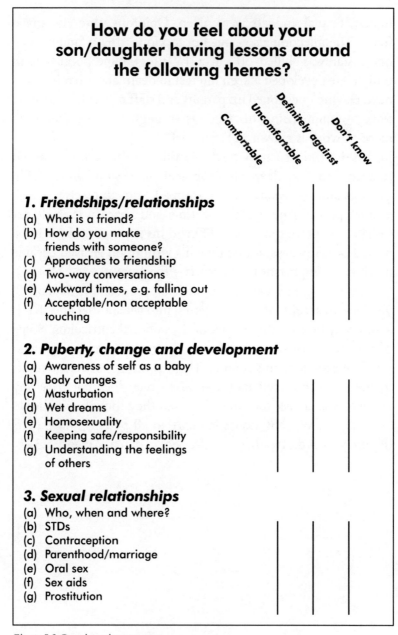

# How do you feel about your son/daughter having lessons around the following themes?

*Comfortable   Uncomfortable   Definitely against   Don't know*

### 1. Friendships/relationships

(a) What is a friend?
(b) How do you make friends with someone?
(c) Approaches to friendship
(d) Two-way conversations
(e) Awkward times, e.g. falling out
(f) Acceptable/non acceptable touching

### 2. Puberty, change and development

(a) Awareness of self as a baby
(b) Body changes
(c) Masturbation
(d) Wet dreams
(e) Homosexuality
(f) Keeping safe/responsibility
(g) Understanding the feelings of others

### 3. Sexual relationships

(a) Who, when and where?
(b) STDs
(c) Contraception
(d) Parenthood/marriage
(e) Oral sex
(f) Sex aids
(g) Prostitution

*Figure 5.2 Questionnaire to parents*

# The Policy

The success of this area of work depends on mutual trust and respect between teaching staff in The Resource and parents. The role of parents in discussing the issues involved in personal and social education with their child is of paramount importance.

The approach to this work will be unified through the lesson plans, yet will be flexibly geared to meet the individual needs of each pupil. Whenever a lesson in PSE has been given, information will be passed to parents about what has been discussed and 'how far' those discussions progressed. This will be done via the dictaphone. Parents will then need to keep staff at The Resource informed of any further discussions that occur at home.

The lessons will usually begin by being teacher-led, but to respect the needs of each individual will often develop into being pupil-led. This will give all pupils the opportunities to come to terms with, and explore further, their own feelings about the changes affecting their lives.

Once the facts about a particular area are given, the pupil may have his own agenda about what he wants to learn from the lessons. This pupil-led content of PSE dictates that we will be moving into many 'grey areas'. For example, it could be difficult to discuss some issues concerning sexuality without looking at the effects of religion, politics and society's attitudes towards the subject. These could be difficult areas for staff in a school in today's society to tackle with confidence. The team of staff in The Resource is a collection of individuals with their own ideas about these issues and how they should be approached with children within an educational context. It is for these reasons that staff have made the following suggestions:

- Each pupil should ideally be given a choice of which member of staff they would prefer to work with on a particular topic. This could change, depending on the topic.

- Each member of staff has the right to curtail a debate/discussion about any topic if they do not feel it appropriate to continue. Parents would be informed if this happened.

- Each member of staff has the right to express his or her own opinion about an issue (if asked directly for it by the pupil), on the understanding that other viewpoints have also been raised and discussed.

- When any group of people discuss issues that could concern the theme of morality and attitudes, mistakes could be made. Staff at The Resource feel it is important to stress that they may make mistakes in what can be a very difficult area of work.

As parents, you have the right in law to withdraw your son/daughter from any lessons in the PSE package involving sex education. There are three broad areas of work around which we would like to formulate lesson plans: friendships, puberty change and development and sexual relationships. Some of these themes will be discussed more than once and fall within all three sections of work. However, it is generally thought that the first section would be covered in Y7 and Y8, the second section in Y8 and Y9, and the final section during Y10 and Y11. Again, it must be stressed that work will be geared to individual need. For example, there may be no perceived advantage in looking at the lesson plan for prostitution unless a pupil has raised the subject or asked specific questions.

I look forward to seeing you at the meeting.

*Figure 5.3 Draft policy*

The returns came back pretty much as we hoped. The overwhelming majority of parents were comfortable with all the themes on the questionnaire. Some areas of PSE for teenagers might be too difficult for parents to manage by themselves and support from school is usually welcomed. This appears to be doubly so for parents of teenagers with autism. The questionnaire gave staff the necessary encouragement to start work on the package.

The package was written with lessons aimed at the varied needs of our pupils. At the 'softer' end the package looks at friendships. This mirrors the type of work carried out at our main feeder school in their social development lessons. It progresses to a large section on puberty, change and development and moves carefully into sexual relationships. Materials were sent for wherever we could find them. A wonderful booklet called '4 Boys' is produced by the Family Planning Association. Of the 20 pupils currently at The Resource, only two are female. At post-16, we have no female students.

The difficulty with a PSE package, especially for teenagers with severe communication disorders, is that it does have to cover everything. Some of our pupils do not have adequate support networks among their mainstream peers. Most of the information and misinformation about sex and relationships is learnt through one's peers. Yet some of our pupils were hearing the odd word and wanting to know what it meant. Slang terms for parts of the sexual anatomy are a further cause of confusion. We had to accept the possibility that some of our pupils might hear expressions relating to oral sex, for example, or prostitution. Where else would we expect and hope for our pupils to come to ask for information and opinions but The Resource, which is crammed full of understanding and accepting adults who can help? We needed to be able to respond appropriately in these situations.

We then invited parents into school one evening to look at the package and policy document, view some of the videos and discuss the approaches we thought appropriate and likely to succeed. It was important to point out to parents that some lessons would only be used with their knowledge and prior approval. It turned out to be a fun evening. Parents went home secure in the knowledge that we were not going to promote homosexuality or the use of sex aids but that we would teach about these issues should it be deemed a pupil needed and had a right to such information and opinions. It was also pointed out that staff had a right not to answer questions on issues they felt uncomfortable about. This type of evening also serves the purpose of bringing parents together. The families we work with live all over Sheffield. Many know each other, but rarely have the opportunity to meet and chat. Staff also got a boost from this meeting because they witnessed at first hand how supportive our group of parents really is. We should not have needed the excuse of discussing a PSE package for this kind of evening to occur and it is something we should do more often.

The work on friendships has to be geared to individual need. Some of our pupils point out their lack of need for friendships, which has to be respected. Tom enjoys sitting with a group of acquaintances, both adults and his peers, and feeling that he is part of the situation. He rarely contributes unless asked a direct question. He does follow the conversation very well because he responds appropriately when asked a direct question. Over the years, Tom has developed the skill of answering direct questions that he does not understand in a neutral manner, for example, by agreeing with the questioner, or by saying that he does not really know. If he has been confused by any question, he will remember this and ask a trusted adult later. At key times during the day, for example, break and dinner time, Tom took to walking across the playing fields on his own. This was his 'chill out' time from the communication bombardment he faced every day. This calm time was encouraged and respected. After several years, Tom was able to share this relaxation activity with another pupil from The Resource. They both appreciated this period of quiet contemplation and a bond of mutual trust developed.

The pupils in The Resource who are diagnosed with Asperger's syndrome are much more likely to want reciprocal friendships than the pupils diagnosed with autism. It can be the pupils with Asperger's syndrome who may have the most difficulties with integration and inclusion. Because of their better language skills in the sense of expressive output, mainstream children in the school generally see these pupils as a bit odd or as the clever bookworm. Mainstream pupils may remember their lessons about autistic spectrum disorders but still have difficulties in reconciling disability with a pupil who is in top set science and maths and sounds to all intents and purposes like an adult. If the same pupil then makes some clumsy attempts at initiating a friendship, or even says 'hello' as he passes an acquaintance, this may be met with hostility or even ridicule. Confusion and depression may be the outcome. Counselling can help and issues around this are discussed in Chapter 4, but other strategies have to be examined. One excellent tool for examining friendships was produced by Marc Segar (1997), *Coping – A Survival Guide for People With Asperger's syndrome.* As he writes: 'It is often difficult to tell the difference between a true friend and a hoax friend but for autistic people, this can be many times harder.' He developed some guidelines, although we have altered some of his original wording, which have proved useful for some pupils in The Resource. Marc's adapted table is shown in Table 5.6 (Marc Segar 1997).

| *Table 5.6 Friendship guidelines* | | |
|---|---|---|
| **True friends** | **Hoax/pretend friends** | **People who do not like you** |
| Treat you the same way as they treat all friends. | May treat you differently from how they treat others. | May ignore you most of the time. |
| Make you feel welcome in the long term as well as the short term. | Might make you feel welcome in the short term and then, later, be impolite or cruel to you. | Will make you feel unwelcome and will notice all your mistakes and may bring them to the attention of other people. |
| If they give you compliments, they will be genuine and sincere. | Might give you compliments, which are *not* genuine. | May give you anything from sarcasm, put-downs and temper tantrums to the silent treatment. |
| Will treat you as an equal. | Might often make unfair requests of you. | Will often treat you as an unimportant person to them. |
| May help you to see the truth behind other people's hoaxes when suitable. | Might want you to make a spectacle of yourself. | May set you up to receive aggression or scorn from others. |
|  | May threaten not to be your friend any more or play on your guilt if it helps them to get their own way. |  |

| What to do | What to do | What to do |
|---|---|---|
| Repay them with the same attention they give you and listen to them. | Stand up to them and don't feel guilty about telling them to p*** off if they have said something which is obviously unfair. | You may have done something to annoy them or they might just be jealous of certain skills or knowledge you have. If it is jealousy, they will *never* admit to it. |
| Accept any compliments they give you by saying 'thank you', and then you won't make them feel silly in any way for having complimented you. | They could be the kind of person who gets pleasure out of hurting people more vulnerable than themselves because they feel weak and inadequate inside. Remember that. | If you find them on their own at any time, they might switch to being quiet and shy towards you. You might be able to question them about why they behave differently to you than they do towards other people. If they can give you a good enough reason, it may be a chance to apologise if you have annoyed them in some way, and say you will try not to annoy them as much in the future. |
| Try to show that you like them by using lots of eye contact. Compliment them on something. | | |

Some of Marc's advice has to be tempered with other considerations, and additions can be made. For example, some mainstream pupils encouraged Jordan to eat grass at lunchtime. Jordan carried out their instructions as he thought these boys were his friends. He came and told staff about this, and we could add this to the list of things that true friends would not do. Pupils are not encouraged to tell other pupils to p*** off however tempting it might be on occasions. They are encouraged to recognise potentially difficult situations and then get some help if they cannot deal with it themselves in a more appropriate manner.

Some of the lessons from Sections Two and Three of the package are outlined below. Lessons One and Two in the section on puberty change and development cover physical changes in the body during adolescence. Terminology for the male and female sex organs is taught. The terms 'erection' and 'wet dreams' are explained. Lesson three moves on swiftly to masturbation (Figure 5.4).

One worksheet for this and other lessons is shown in Figure 5.5.

# Masturbation

Aims

(a) To provide pupils (male and female) with knowledge of what masturbation is and how it is achieved.

(b) To provide instruction and advice on suitable places for masturbation to occur.

(c) To discuss any myths or worries that arise about masturbation.

(d) To provide time to discuss feelings and concerns.

Resources
Video, **Living and Growing** (produced by Channel 4).

## Method

The facts will be given in a non-judgemental way. It is likely that the following areas would be discussed:

- Explanation of what masturbation means, i.e. deliberate touching and stroking of the sex organs.
- Ejaculation.
- Slang terms used.
- Is it normal if you do? Is it normal if you don't?
- How often do males/females masturbate?
- Where are the most suitable and safe places to masturbate, i.e. where you will not be disturbed/interrupted?
- Is it okay to imagine/fantasise?
- Is masturbation sinful or morally wrong?
- Can masturbation be harmful to your health?

## Evaluation

1. Questionnaire.
2. Worksheets.

*Figure 5.4 Masturbation*

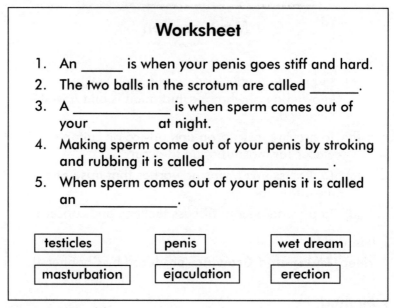

*Figure 5.5 PSE worksheet*

After participating in some of these PSE lessons, Tom went home to talk through some of the issues with his parents. Tom and his father went for some long walks together at the weekend to give time and space for discussion to take place. Tom was fortunate to have such honest and open parents, but even they had to establish one rule quite early on. It was made clear to Tom that these were talks he could have with Mum, Dad or staff at The Resource. Under no circumstances was Tom to expect his grandmother to become involved in discussing issues about puberty and adolescence. In an environment of honesty and high expectations, Tom could understand some of the differences in attitudes to sexual matters between his parents and his grandparents' generation – insight indeed.

Section three of the PSE package looks at issues surrounding sexual relationships. One of the key lessons that has to be taught and retaught is in the vital area of keeping safe. This is particularly important for some of our pupils who are out of school on work placements. However, the section begins with the age-old questions of who, when and where (Figure 5.6).

---

# Who, when and where?

## Aim
To provide information within a legal framework about sexual relationships.

## Resources
Pens and paper. Problem pages. Worksheets.

## Methods
The teaching methods used for this section will be:
- discussion
- role play
- worksheets.

The subject area naturally divides into three subsections: who, when, where?

## Who?
Teaching will focus primarily on the issue of **consent**. It will examine:
- the meaning of consent
- the individual's rights concerning his or her own body
- the individual's right to say 'no'
- the age of legal consent.

It is anticipated that with some students this will involve the discussion of issues surrounding the age of consent for homosexuals. Information will be provided within a legal framework, but will be essentially presented within a non-judgemental approach. Having established the importance of consent, the lessons will examine issues sur-

---

rounding 'without consent'. This will include rape and under-age sex.

### When?
Teaching will continue to focus on consent. In addition, it will emphasis the need for **maturity**. It will focus on:
- real life
- mutual involvement
- trust, safety, certainty and maturity.

This section will emphasise the importance of **thought** and **consideration**. It will stress the need to **avoid impulsive actions** and the importance of **talking things through**. Real life scenarios or storylines from TV soap operas will be used as a basis for discussion.

### Where?
Teaching will focus on the concept of **privacy**. It will explain the term privacy and discuss 'ideal' situations for sex in terms of safety, security and comfort. As in the other areas, it will be stressed that this is an issue which is to be decided by the two people involved, having first **assessed** the risk of the situation. It may be necessary to discuss legal differences between homosexual and heterosexual sex. It is expected that discussion will occur, but that some pupils may require clear-cut rules and guidance in this area.

### Evaluation
- 'Real life' scenario worksheets
- Tick sheets

*Figure 5.6 Who, when and where?*

- Fictitious problem page worksheets

An example of a simple tick sheet used for one assessment in this area is shown in Figure 5.7. It provides the basis for further discussion and debate. Humour is important in creating a relaxed and informal environment in which such debates can occur.

# Worksheet

Listed below are some places where people might think about having sexual intercourse with their partner. Tick the boxes when you decide whether sexual intercourse in these places might be:

✓ OK

✓ Not OK

✓ Perhaps

Pupil's name:

Date:

| Place | OK | Not OK | Perhaps |
|---|---|---|---|
| In the cinema | | | |
| In your bedroom | | | |
| On a busy beach | | | |
| On a secluded (very private) beach | | | |
| In the supermarket | | | |
| In a car | | | |
| In the living room | | | |
| At a bus stop | | | |
| On a bus | | | |
| In the bathroom | | | |
| At your friend's house | | | |
| At your auntie's house | | | |
| In the countryside | | | |
| In the garden | | | |

Figure 5.7 Evaluation of 'the where'

Evaluation of PSE lessons is a difficult area and one that needs to be approached with creativity. Tick charts have their place, but assessment does need to be meaningful and age-appropriate as well as demonstrating that the pupil has a grasp of the issues which have been taught and discussed. One good way of doing this is by writing teenage magazine-type problems for the pupil to respond to. Some of these from each of the three sections of our PSE package are shown in Figures 5.8, 5.9 and 5.10.

These problem pages make the pupil feel like the expert. Their written responses are generally very mature in the advice they give, and factually correct. Our pupils may not get a job as an agony aunt or uncle, but their responses give staff some proof that they have understood the lessons in the PSE package.

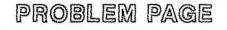

I'm going to sound like a real cry-baby, but my problem has been making me miserable. I don't have any real friends. There are people I say hello to, but no one I can call a special friend. Other people have four or five friends. I am always by myself. Please help.

**Peter from London**

I'm being teased by my friends at school. They say I'm stupid, and I'm starting to believe them.
They criticise what I wear and what I say. It's been going on for weeks. I feel like running away.

John from Oxford

There's a new girl in my class at school. I really want to talk to her 'cause she seems like she might be good fun. I don't know how to start it, or what to say.

Gary from Ipswich

*Figure 5.8 Problem page*

# PROBLEM PAGE

I am 14 years old. I woke up this morning to find I had wet the bed. It did not smell of urine. What is happening to me and what should I do?

My Dad says it is wrong to touch my penis. He says that if I have a wank, I will go blind. Is this true? What should I do?

Adam from Devon

I have just learnt how to masturbate. The thing is, I want to do it every day. Is this strange? Are there any rules       about

A girl saw me touching my private parts through my trousers in the middle of a Maths lesson. Now she is telling everyone that I am strange. What shall I do?

Jake from Birmingham

*Figure 5.9 Problem page*

# PROBLEM PAGE

My mates say I'm soft because I've been going out with this girl for three weeks. Every time I try to 'touch her up' she stops me. They say she's really dying to have sex with me, and that I should just force her. They say that girls like a bloke to be strong and that when girls say 'no' they really mean 'yes'. Am I really the wimp they say I am?

Softie – Bradford

I've been going out with my girlfriend for five months now. We're both sixteen and we're really in love. We've kissed a lot and she lets me feel her breasts. How will I know when it is the right time to go further? I would really like to have sex, but I'm afraid I'll scare her off.

Perfect timing - Cardiff

We're both 17, but Bill says he wants to wait to have sex until we're older and more mature. I think we're old enough now. Which one of us is right?

In a hurry – Bognor

I'm 14 and in love. I want to have sex with my 18-year-old boyfriend but he's too scared. He says that if anyone finds out, then he will be put in prison for raping me. I don't believe this because I'm willing to have sex with him. Is he right?

Under age: London

*Figure 5.10 Problem page*

It is always interesting to see the reaction of OFSTED inspectors when they see the lessons on homosexuality or prostitution. However, we have only had positive reactions from these people. They cannot be given any room to find a weakness in what has been developed. Policies must be in place, proper consultation with parents must have occurred, lessons and evaluations must be well written with good materials to support them. Which OFSTED inspector is going to argue with you, if these issues have been dealt with professionally, competently and with the needs of the pupils as the guiding factor? Few will argue if parents have been properly consulted through questionnaires and meetings.

It must be stressed again that space and time has to be created to allow for pupil-led PSE/life projects. One of our severely autistic pupils had a wonderful vision of being married to a beautiful woman, having a candlelit dinner with her on the balcony of some romantic and exotic Mediterranean island and plying her with expensive gifts. A symphony of violins would be heard drifting on the warm balmy evening air. His rigidity of thought was such that he believed everyone got married. Worse than that, he believed everyone who got married was blissfully happy. Staff could not ignore this, and, in the nicest possible way, felt it important to challenge this picture.

The pupil would not be convinced by staff in The Resource about issues connected with marriage. It was suggested to the pupil that he devise a questionnaire to give to all staff in the school about marriage. With support he was able to do this. Our wonderful mainstream colleagues returned their questionnaires with great speed. The pupil was able to assimilate the information contained and could clearly see that not everyone was married and that age was not the only deciding factor in this. He could read about the good parts of being married, but also about the not so good bits. We were able to extend this work by arranging some interviews with married and single staff in the school. The pupil relished being the interviewer and prepared some excellent questions. His rigid outlook on marriage has gradually changed.

He was guided from the 'black and white' into the messy grey area in which we all have to operate.

Teaching and learning is always at its very best when it is pupil-led. If the system is not flexible enough to allow this, then the system needs to be changed. Our children need to be given time and respect so that they can teach us about what they want to learn. Their autism and their style of learning must be respected. However, we are not passive players in this process. It is vital to have packages of lessons available to staff which are easy to use and evaluate. These lessons must take the pupil into areas s/he would be denied if it were left to the national curriculum. They must be used flexibly to suit the needs of the individual. At its best, this is a two-way process in which pupils and staff alike have lessons to learn about each other.

# 6

# Integration into Work

Integration into Work is a rather grand title for another part of our curriculum. It is one of the parts that appears to interest people the most. The theoretical framework for Integration into Work is based on common sense and the accepted knowledge that children with ASD learn better in real life situations. There were several factors that prompted staff to begin what we thought would be a minor alteration to the curriculum offered to our pupils.

First, it was felt that to have a good model of access and inclusion just up to the age of 16 in a secondary school was not enough. Remembering the people and parents who were instrumental in fighting for the right of our Resource to exist in the first place, staff felt that we would only be playing at inclusion if everything came to a standstill at 16. Access and inclusion is for life, or should be. There are examples of adults with autism or Asperger's syndrome who have received good support and services after the age of 16, both in further education and from social services. Marc Fleisher is one such person in the UK. However, these examples, despite being inspirational and providing a superb insight into the condition, are only relevant if they can be replicated on a larger scale. Staff began to question people they knew who worked in the public and private sectors to see how many adults with autism were in their workplace. The reliable questionnaire was sent out to about 50 firms, large and small, to see if they employed anyone with a severe communication disorder, or if they had any knowledge about the strengths such people could offer in the employment market. A working group within Sheffield City Council came up with the depressing figure of a 95 per cent unemployment rate among adults with any kind of learning disability. Adults with autism were included in this horrific figure. Of the few questionnaires returned, the outlook in terms of employment looked bleak. Yet we knew our pupils had tremendous potential to offer certain types of employers. We looked to our colleagues in the USA to see wonderful examples of supported employment schemes. The UK would appear to be many years behind in this type of work.

For a short while, the enormity of this situation was too much for staff to contemplate. By this time (1996) staff were working closely with ten pupils. Our intake was established as four pupils a year. Demand for our provision far outstripped the number of available places. What point was there in developing a model of inclusion in a school that finished abruptly at the ages of 16 or 18 if good college provision could be found? It was felt that we had two choices. First, we could do something to prepare our pupils for a 95 per cent chance that they would experience unemployment. Second, we could attempt to understand why this was happening and think of how we could help remedy the situation. We could have added the lessons about signing on for housing benefit, disability living allowance and job seeker's allowance to our life skills package, but it was strongly felt that the majority of our pupils should be in paid employment as adults. Staff in The Resource, I am proud to say, are a stubborn group of people and if an idea becomes regarded as a human right, the poor teacher in charge knows he has work to do. Put another way, show us the mountain and we'll attempt to climb it. All of that sounds a little altruistic. At the centre of our concern is a group of young people who are brilliant in certain areas. The 'peak and trough' profile of skills for a person with autism has so many positive features. Playing to these skill areas was something staff were used to doing at school. Utilising these same strengths in terms of employment seemed like common sense.

We were discovering at first hand on a daily basis the tremendous strengths of people with ASD, when given the right structure, guidance and support. If an employer wanted someone who would take great delight in getting all the labels on tins of baked beans facing the correct way on a supermarket shelf, then we knew just the pupil for that job. If 50,000 letters needed to be enveloped at speed, we knew the pupil who would do that better than any 'regular' person. If an employer needed someone to memorise the whereabouts of 30,000 files and check these against microfiche records, we felt that we knew just that person. If employers were looking for people who would have excellent attendance and punctuality records, they need look no further than someone with autism. Given the right support and guidance, our pupils would make brilliant employees, and would not leave what others might consider a mundane and repetitive job after six months. It was felt that the structure of school and post-16 education should be replaced by the structure of employment, ideally full time and paid, but we would also consider part-time or voluntary work for our pupils. Something had to be done. The need was tangible. The boundaries had to be pushed back and employers had to wake up, smell the coffee and realise they were missing out. Inclusion in education had benefits for all parties involved. Increasing the representation of people with autistic disorders in the employment marketplace also must have benefits for all concerned.

There are other groups involved in attempting to improve the situation concerning employment for people with disabilities. We did not know this at the time. As we have progressed, people from these organisations have come to us and shared their knowledge and experience. One such body is the Employers' Forum on Disability. In a promotional booklet, 'Unlocking Potential' (Scott-Parker and Zadek 2000), the case for including disabled people in the workforce is outlined:

1.  Disabled people are as productive and reliable as any other employees.

2.  In living their day-to-day lives, many disabled people develop transferable problem-solving skills that are invaluable in the workplace.

3.  Disabled people in work tend to have better attendance records, stay with employers longer and have fewer accidents at work.

4.  Government support is often available should workplace adjustments be needed to enable business to realise the potential of disabled people.

5.  The spending power of disabled people and their families in the UK is estimated at an annual £45–50 billion.

6.  Staff morale and team development are enhanced when businesses are seen to be good employers of people with disabilities.

Scott-Parker and Zadek conclude by saying that organisations which have successfully employed disabled people are keen to employ more. So why is there such a massive unemployment rate among adults with autism? First, if we assume that the majority of the population remains unsure about the disability of autism, then there is no reason why employers should be any different. No one could expect employers to come to us and ask about the strengths which people with autism may have.

The second difficulty was that in secondary schools across the country this need to place pupils with an employer, to give them vital and varied experience, was already recognised. A two-week block of work experience is permitted and in most schools actively encouraged for pupils in Year 10. We could look forward to these two weeks in Y10 and make them as beneficial as possible for our pupils. That could have been it. We were an integrated provision and would now presumably have access to these two weeks of work experience. However, for our pupils in The Resource, this was too little and too late.

By the time Year 9 comes to an end for our pupils, with the rigours of SATS, we know roughly what grades to expect from GCSEs. This is not an exact science, but an area we improve at every year. For those pupils who are aiming to get the E and F grades, we did not want to plough on through three further years of the national curriculum only to achieve these grades. It would not be enough for potential employers to sit up and take notice. Staff in The Resource did not want to wait until Y10 for these pupils to experience the world of employment. Our idea was to look for some possible work experience placements from Y9 and on a regular basis, for example, one morning or afternoon each week. However, those pupils who might be more likely to achieve higher grades at GCSE would have to be omitted from the scheme. We did not want to jeopardise the D to A grades at GCSE because these are already valued and recognised by employers. One further reason for wanting a regular placement with an employer is because The Resource has pupils who would only just be starting to settle into a placement after the two-week block in Y10. The too little, too late argument was accepted as fact.

With our usual naivety, over 50 packages of information were sent to local employers about what the problem was and what we proposed to do about it with their assistance. A tremendous amount of time and effort went into these packages of information. They were followed up with telephone calls two weeks later. The response was dismal. There is no doubt in my mind that most of these 50 packages of information were filed under 'B' for bin. This was extremely demoralising, but probably stemmed from the fact that The Resource is a small organisation and at that time had little credibility in this area of work. I cringe when any company attempts to 'cold sell' me something over the telephone or at the front door, so we could hardly be too depressed at a poor response to our equivalent efforts.

However, one follow-up phone call to the supermarket giant, Sainsbury's, brought a half-decent reply. A personnel manager offered me a 15-minute appointment to meet with her at a store about two miles from the school. This personnel manager no longer works for the store and I do not know where she is now. But this one person started the journey of enabling employers to see that our pupils are worthy of a chance. How often do changes in the fabric of our society begin with one person being willing to listen and open their minds to a possibility? I had a lovely meeting with her and was shown around the huge supermarket. Everyone was so friendly that I could easily picture one of our pupils working at Sainsbury's. The canteen served wonderful snacks and meals and the pupil I had in mind would enjoy this aspect of the job. The personnel manager asked some valid questions and said that she would need a little time to think about what would be the best area of the store for this pupil to work in. She would then liaise with the people in this area and explain about the project. I left Sainsbury's 'on a high'. Wherever that personnel manager is now, I hope she is happy and successful because she deserves to be.

The personnel manager quickly called The Resource with the superb news that one Y9 pupil could work at Sainsbury's for one morning a week with full-time support from a member of staff from The Resource – me! The pupil and I had a brilliant time. Other arrangements had to be made such as organising transport to the work placement in the morning. Parental support was quickly received. I could train the pupil in the use of public transport for the return journey back to school for afternoon lessons. The most appropriate department within the busy store had to be educated and encouraged to produce a suitable work schedule for the pupil. The shift was from 9am until 12 midday with a 15-minute tea break halfway through. Sainsbury's provided a free lunch for the pupil and his support worker, which was excellent. It was a long time since I had experienced the simple pleasure of a 15-minute tea break. We had to receive training in the art of displaying 'produce' (fruit and vegetables to the lay person). We were also shown a series of videos about what to do in the event of fire, health and safety issues and advice on customer courtesy. The staff at Sainsbury's literally had to push me back to school because I would have happily worked there long after the time when Andrew actually needed me. All the staff were so kind and helpful. Andrew's story is told in greater detail in Chapter 9. However, his story was only going to be the start of the programme. Andrew could not remain as just one more isolated example of innovation and good practice.

The effect on this pupil was remarkable. The morning we spent together at Sainsbury's quickly became the highlight of his week (and mine). He spent his weekends visiting other supermarkets and comparing them to the store he worked in. He bought promotional literature back to school and kept a diary of his placement. His self-identity was born. His mother shopped at the store while her son worked on fruit and vegetables. We were so pleased with the pupil and ourselves that we wanted more employers to hear about the success. Life had never been better for Andrew and we wanted to sing about it from the rooftops. What better way than to talk to the local newspapers? This was a human story concerning an employer who could become a leading light for us in this area of work. Employers would read about this brilliant scheme and want to duplicate it in their own setting. The story appeared in the two main Sheffield newspapers. We quickly sent out our package of information again to the same employers, but this time with press cuttings about Andrew and Sainsbury's. That is when our problems began. A lovely man in a grey suit appeared at The Resource a week after the article in the press informing me in the nicest possible way that we were breaking the law. Our naivety had got us into real trouble. The 1973 Employment Act (or something similar) states that work experience can only occur in Y10 and has to be restricted to two weeks out of the year. We were lawbreakers on two charges. Headlines of a different nature flashed before my eyes, concerning the end of my career.

This law is in place for the excellent reason of preventing exploitation of children by employers. We should have researched the legal aspect of this project before starting. The man in the grey suit insisted that Andrew's placement would have to be changed from work experience to work shadowing: that is, he could watch other people work but do none of the tasks himself. This was difficult to explain to Andrew but we did give it a try. Sainsbury's were wonderful yet again and moved Andrew to different parts of the supermarket so he could get a better overview of their operations. However, his frustration and disappointment began to grow. We were devastated and so were Andrew's parents, but determined not to give in without a fight.

In desperation, we turned to the then Opposition Minister for Education, David Blunkett. Letters outlining the events were written and within three days he responded with a phone call to my home. I was impressed not only by his prompt response to my letter, but by the way he made me realise that he had grasped the importance of this case.

Two weeks later, I was called to attend a meeting with some officers from the education department in Sheffield. I was told that with certain conditions concerning paperwork the scheme could continue as a pilot study for two years. A further discussion took place about calling the scheme something other than work experience. Presumably this was to prevent us falling foul of the law and ending up in court with the nice man in the grey suit. Much of the manoeuvring did not interest me, as long as these people were happy and left us alone to get on with things. The council's solicitor became involved and decided on the term 'Integration into Work'. Integration into Work differs from work experience in name only, but everyone appeared happy and we could get on with this area of our curriculum. I have never discovered the role that David Blunkett played in this whole episode, but he has been kept up to date with our work ever since. Whatever political opinions were involved, we were right to ask for his help, and I would like to think that we have justified his faith in us.

Four years later, the scheme is successful. Not all of our pupils have access to Integration into Work. Our more academically gifted pupils cannot miss one morning each week of their lessons. These pupils complain bitterly about not having access to this part of the curriculum. They have to be content with the two-week block of work experience in Y10. However, the majority of our pupils begin on the scheme in Year 9. The search for suitable and appropriate employers has become slightly easier, but only just. Articles in the press have raised the profile of the scheme, but it is perhaps still too different for 'the establishment' to comprehend. The most common reason for polite

---

# Integration into Work
# A Policy Document

## Background

The unemployment rate in Sheffield for adults with learning disabilities is approximately 95 per cent. Included in this figure are adults with severe communication/language disorders. The reasons for this unacceptable level of unemployment are complex, but several factors seem to be central to the issue:

1. The majority of employers do not have practical experience or knowledge about young adults with communication/language disorders.

2. The basis of a mainstream education occurs in the classroom. Practical experience of the work environment is permitted in Y10, but then only for a two-week period. For most pupils with severe communication/language disorders, this is too little, too late.

3. Pupils with severe communication disorders learn in different ways from their mainstream peers.

Our pupils learn in practical and visual ways. Abstract concepts and verbal teaching/explanations will not usually work as well.

### Aims of the project

(a) To place each Y9, Y10 and Y11 pupil with a local employer for one morning/afternoon each week throughout the year.

(b) To support these placements with a member of staff until such time as the employer feels confident enough to manage the situation with either reduced support, or monthly visits from the staff member.

(c) To write aims for each placement and to link these closely to the pupil's Statement of Special Educational Need.

(d) To carry out a risk assessment for each placement.

(e) To give the employer written information about the pupil with areas of strength/weakness and suggestions. This information will be distributed to other employees who come into contact with the pupil on placement.

(f) To encourage the employer to give a written reference when a pupil finishes on a placement.

### Safety

Every possible way of making Integration into Work as risk free as possible will be examined. Risk assessments will be carried out with each employer. A member of staff from The Resource will visit each potential placement to look at health and safety issues and to discuss the placement with the employer. Initially, a member of staff will give full support and for some pupils it may be necessary to keep this in place throughout the year. However, for the majority of pupils, the aim will be to increase independ-ence while on the placement. This will be carried out on a gradual basis. Employers will be instructed to phone The Resource if there is something they are not sure about. Training will be given on the use of public transport if this is appropriate. The pupils are insured while on their placement.

### Conclusion

Integration into Work has taken over a year to become es-tablished. It has the potential to break new ground in the area of education, training and employment. The ultimate number of pupils on placements could be twelve. For this to happen we would need financial support for the scheme if it were to continue.

Doubts and worries about the scheme will always continue and if any parent did not want their son/daughter to be involved, this would be respected. It is impossible to summarise the benefits of Integration into Work on paper in a policy document like this. I would urge parents and professionals to talk to people from the three groups who are vital to the success of this scheme, to hear their opinions: parents with a child already on the scheme, employers and the pupils themselves.

*Figure 6.1 Integration into work*

refusals remains the age of the pupils. The policy for the scheme, which was sent to all parents, is shown in Figure 6.1.

Each employer receives a document outlining aims for the placement, and full-time support for as long as they and the pupil require it. Information is given about the pupil. An example of in-formation provided about a pupil is shown in Figure 6.2. An example of the aims for one pupil on a placement is shown in Figure 6.3.

# Information about Joe Pretend for Staff at Employment Placement Y

## Introduction

Joe has difficulties in the area of communication that involve the understanding and use of verbal language. That means he may take longer to process any spoken language and derive meaning from it. A simple request or instruction may put Joe under pressure, especially if he does not know the other person very well.

## Areas of strength

Joe is becoming more confident as he realises that he has a lot to offer. He is independent at school for about 35 per cent of his week. He takes pride in this independence and responds well to praise. Joe is becoming increasingly aware of the difficulties he faces and is getting better at explaining how he is feeling. Joe learns new practical tasks very quickly. He likes routine and once he is clear about a task, he will work extremely hard.

## Support

Joe will be with you for one morning a week. Initially, a member of staff from The Resource will come with Joe to help him and you get a work routine or schedule established. If you have any questions or suggestions concerning Joe, please do not hesitate to talk to the member of staff with him. The aim is for Joe to become independent for this one morning a week with you. This will not happen until Joe is happy about the situation, and you as the staff feel that he knows what he should be doing. In other words, Joe will not be left without support until he can do the job satisfactorily.

### *Suggestions*

1. Joe is desperate not to do anything that makes him stand out as being 'different'. He is fearful of being singled out if he fails to achieve a set objective. In this respect, gentle words of encouragement and guidance are the only way forward. Any harsh words could reduce Joe to tears and damage his newly emerging self-esteem.

2. If Joe is clear about the task, he will work hard. From time to time he may need gentle reminders to remain on task, but then, don't we all! He will accept these prompts to stay on task in good spirit.

3. Complex sentences and detailed explanations will not make the task any easier for Joe; they will only serve to confuse him even further. It is difficult to understand this feeling, but imagine it like being spoken to in a language of which you only have a limited understanding. Joe needs brief and simple explanations of what is expected of him. Once he is clear about the task, it is as if the 'lightbulb' above his head comes on. His response will often be, 'Oh I get it now.'

4. The use of written material will greatly assist Joe. If he can see the jobs you want him to do written in a list, he will be much clearer about your expectations of him.

5. Occasional checks are needed to see whether Joe has really understood the instruction/task.

6. Joe responds well to routine. The ideal would be for Joe to have a number of tasks that he completes each week. Once this routine is established, new tasks can be introduced gradually to extend his knowledge and expertise.

Joe is making tremendous progress at school, both academically and socially. His self-esteem continues to improve, and he is well liked by teachers and his peers. He is a joy to work with. Thank you for your time and patience, and for the opportunity given to Joe. We have every confidence that Joe will become an asset to you.

*Figure 6.2 Pupil information supplied to employer*

## Joe Pretend
## Aims for Integration into Work

**Placement**:          Supermarket Y.

**Date**:          Oct. 1996 to July 1997.

**Frequency**:          Every Monday morning 9am to12.30pm

**Transport**:          Morning – Parents. Afternoon – independent travel on 97A bus to school.

### *The following aims are quoted from Joe's Statement of SEN.*

1. Continuing attention to developing social interaction skills.
2. Strategies to maintain self-confidence and self-esteem (Section III of Joe's Statement dated 5.8.94).

### *Aims of the placement*

(a) To develop the concept of time as being important in the work environment.
(b) To experience working as part of a team.
(c) To carry out instructions given by Joe's line manager.

(d) To develop an ability to use his own initiative.

(e) To enjoy the social times of tea break and lunchtimes in the staff canteen.

(f) To be able to use public transport for the return journey to school.

(g) To be able to respond appropriately to customers when they ask any questions.

(h) To learn about health and safety issues at work.

(i) To develop the ability to work consistently over a period of time.

(j) For Joe to develop into an asset to supermarket Y as a work student.

*Figure 6.3 Pupil aims supplied to employer*

At the end of the year, an evaluation is written and the employer is encouraged to give a written reference for the pupil's Record of Achievement. If the placement has been successful for all parties, we tentatively suggest that it would be lovely if the pupil could remain with the employer for the next year. The responses improve each year.

One employer, a local garden centre, took over a year to decide to join the scheme. Having been gently persuaded that we did know what we were doing, Steve was placed during his Y9. He had support for his first six mornings. The pupil loved every minute of his morning a week (despite suffering from hay fever). He quickly became independent on the placement and in travelling back to school using public transport. He returned one lunchtime after his three-hour shift with a huge grin on his face. After some questioning, he proudly announced that he had carried some plants to the car of a customer. She had given him a £1 tip. This person had no idea what effect this had on our pupil. After the first year, I phoned the owner of the garden centre to ask meekly if the pupil could continue with his placement during his

Y10. The owner was horrified that Steve might be removed from the placement. In her opinion, Steve had become part of their team. Steve is well respected by his work colleagues. He is now well into his third year at the garden centre. I would expect him to leave there with glowing references. Future employers will have to take this into consideration alongside the E and D grades Steve is capable of at GCSE. Steve may not choose to pursue horticulture at post-16, but he will have had three years of experience in a busy and demanding employment setting.

The range of employers that have been encouraged to offer our pupils a placement has gradually extended over the four years of the scheme. Retail is a key sector because of the routine nature of some of the tasks. We have had, and in most cases still have, pupils on placements at the Co-op, Marks and Spencer and Tesco. After one article in a local newspaper, the manager of a café in a nearby park telephoned The Resource to offer a placement. Three of our pupils had successful placements working in this café. It is always pleasing when employers offer a placement rather than staff having to ask. Other pupils have worked in a local library, a daycare centre for elderly people, a large insurance company, a bakery and a health club. However, there will always be more placements to find to suit individual need. Rachel would like to work with animals and we are experiencing great difficulty in finding her a suitable employer.

On occasions, it is more suitable for a pupil to have some experience of the world of work within the school setting first. Staff may feel that a pupil is not quite ready for a placement with an 'outside' employer. One pupil worked for a morning a week in the school library learning a variety of tasks. The school librarian proved to be an excellent teacher and guide for this pupil. In his Y10, the same pupil was ready to take up a placement in the local community library. The school librarian wrote a reference for this pupil to take to the local community library. Another pupil followed in his footsteps and has been at the library for two years.

There are always difficulties that arise on placements. It is impossible to predict where and when they will arise, but it is vital that someone can get to the place of employment quickly. What seem to be dire emergencies for our employers are usually difficulties that it takes an experienced colleague about five minutes to solve. Common-sense ideas can be applied within the framework of knowledge about autism.

Sean had full support at a large insurance company for the first eight months of his placement. He worked in a busy filing department. Sean learnt how to envelope letters and deliver the internal post. This branch of the company has about 1000 employees. It was the task of enveloping letters that caused an initial difficulty once Sean became independent on the placement. A telephone call was taken in The Resource from Sean's line manager. He was suggesting that if Sean carried on working at such a fast rate while putting letters in envelopes, his department would be facing redundancies. This line manager wondered if we could teach Sean the 'English work ethic' of working hard for a while and then taking it a little steadier. This is a very advanced skill and although the line manager's comments were said 'tongue in cheek' it was vital for us to respond in some way. My colleague who first supported Sean made an immediate visit to the company to assess the situation. It quickly became clear to him where the problem was. This line manager and his team of staff were so efficient and kind that they organised Sean's workload and got everything ready for his arrival at 9am. Sean had his own desk and as soon as he walked in all he could see were the thousand letters and thousand envelopes for him to fill. Sean is a pupil who will not rest until a task is completed. He could see that 1000 letters needed folding and putting in 1000 envelopes. Sean did this with great speed and efficiency. Nothing would distract him from this mission. No discussions could take place with colleagues because Sean had work to do.

My colleague made the suggestion to Sean's line manager that perhaps 200 letters and envelopes could be put on his desk, with the others being hidden out of sight. Having completed 200, Sean could be sent to make a coffee, and preferably make other people a drink as well. Then the next 200 letters and envelopes could be put on Sean's desk. The whole process would slow Sean down and also serve to reduce some of the stress that Sean might feel. Everyone was happy. For Sean, it meant that staff at the company grew more confident about teaching him new tasks. He learnt to use the photocopier and fax machine. He learnt how to check a file on microfiche with the paper file to ensure that both copies matched. Sean could do this faster than anyone in the office. All he had to do was write down the reference numbers of any pages that were missing. This might be considered a repetitive and mundane task for a 'regular' person. This company (along with many others) experiences a high turnover of young staff. Sean loved the work and had three superb years with this company. They gave him the company sweatshirt to wear. Sean drew some of his train pictures (like the one on the front cover of this book), which were displayed on the office walls. Staff in the office bought Sean birthday and Christmas presents including a video of vintage steam trains. Sean's mother visited the office to meet staff. The whole experience was extremely positive for all parties. With a short break from the scheme, this employer is prepared to take a second pupil on placement within the same department.

As usual, some of the mistakes made turn out to be valuable learning experiences. Terry was about to start work in an elderly people's daycare centre. He was apprehensive about what he might have in common with people over the age of 70. I told him that he needed to think about his strong interest in history and relate that to the elderly people. What I should have done, given more time, was role-play some possible conversations with Terry. My teaching should have been much more specific. On our first morning, Terry sat next to a frail looking elderly man and said, 'So then, what did you do in the war?' Before I had time to intervene or apologise, the elderly man replied that he had worked as an engineer in the navy on submarines. Terry and this man went on to have a wonderful conversation about World War II. I sat down, a quivering wreck, and quietly drank my mug of cocoa.

Integration into Work has to be supported by work in The Resource. Things such as stock rotation (moving stock with an earlier use-by date near to the front of the display) need to be reinforced and practised. Placing numbered files in order from smallest to largest when each has six digits can easily be practised away from the work environment. Worksheets can be used to look at risk or health and safety issues. Practical examples can be used like putting up signs saying 'Danger Slippery Floors' when a pupil has mopped the classroom.

We also have lessons on keeping safe. Integration into Work places young pupils in potentially dangerous situations. Many of our pupils could be vulnerable to verbal, emotional or sexual exploitation. They must be taught how to be assertive, and what the correct procedures are if anyone should try to make inappropriate suggestions to them. Assessments can be made using the 'problem type page' used in teenage magazines (examples of these are described in Chapter 5). These types of lesson need revisiting on a regular basis.

A mainstream secondary school and the world of work are two potentially difficult and hostile environments for people with autism. Our pupils do have worries and anxieties just as we all do. However, for someone with autism these worries can be much more powerfully felt than by a 'regular' person. Time spent in social isolation could exacerbate anxiety levels. Discussion and an atmosphere of openness, warmth and security can help pupils to talk about worries, but sometimes a little more is required in the way of structure.

Tom experienced some stressful times during his Y9. Worries and anxieties dominated his thoughts. He had developed a fantasy world and was showing increasing signs of withdrawing into this world on a more regular basis, both at school and home.

Talking about these worries (some of which were about his work placement in a supermarket) only appeared to heighten his anxiety levels. The supermarket Tom worked in for one morning a week is very small and the gap between aisles is narrow. Stocking shelves is not easy when customers are trying to get on with their shopping. Tom had knocked a couple of items off the shelf or dropped something. His anxieties and the fantasy world were beginning to get out of control.

Using our limited knowledge of autism, staff thought it might help if we could structure the worries in some way. We also needed to timetable these worries so that Tom could know when was an appropriate time to discuss any issues he had. The idea of a 'worry programme' became established. We have used this sheet with two pupils and I feel that its use could be widened. One example is shown in Figure 6.4.

These worry plans could be as simple or detailed as you need to suit the individual. It is important that worries are timetabled so as not to take up too much precious teaching time. These plans could be completed on the computer. It must be satisfying to throw away or tear up a worry plan when there is no longer a need for it. Alternatively, a pupil could have six or more worry plans open and active at any one time. However, if 15 minutes is given to each plan in a week, this structure is at least enabling staff to manage the worries and anxieties. For some pupils in The Resource, writing things down does appear to relieve tension.

Not all of our students at post-16 chose to pursue courses that are related in some way to the work experience they have enjoyed at pre-16. Post-16 provision is discussed in more detail in Chapter 8. However, two pupils from The Resource who had work placements in supermarkets have progressed to taking courses in retail at college. One pupil who had a placement in a café and one in a bakery wanted to do a course in bakery at post-16. However, one pupil who had a successful placement at an elderly people's daycare centre has decided not to pursue a course at post-16 relevant to this area of employment. He is

# Worry Plan

Name:....................... Date:............... Time:...........

| |
|---|
| I am worried because<br><br><br>Is it a big worry? Yes/No/Don't know |
| Where and when can I discuss my worry? |
| Who can I discuss my worry with? |
| The worry |
| What are my options? |

I am not worried about this now.
    Yes/No

I need to discuss it again.
    Yes/No

I can throw this plan away.
    Yes/No

I want to keep it.
    Yes /No

When and where?

With?

Staff initials ................... Signed .......................

*Figure 6.4 Worry plan*

doing NVQ Level 2 in Office and Administration. This student looks back with great fondness to his year on placement at the daycare centre, but he also had a year of mornings in the school library followed by a year in the local community library. Office and administrative work will suit him just fine.

Integration into Work has achieved what it set out to do: offering a more broad and balanced curriculum for the majority of our pupils. However, it has done more than that because the 12 employers we have worked with in the last four years are now more knowledgeable and experienced in the field of autism. Staff from The Resource have learnt first hand about different sectors of the employment market. Learning and experiencing what other people go through in their job is a vital part of integration, inclusion and access. It always has to be a two-way process. Staff try to understand and empathise with mainstream teachers at school. They also have to understand and empathise with the management and workforce at Sainsbury's, the local café, garden centre, library and large insurance company. Employers have witnessed at first hand pupils with autism doing a job of work and doing it well. The fellow employees of our pupils have experienced working alongside someone with autism. It could have been their first experience of someone with autism. Without exception, this first experience for them is a positive one. However, the scheme has highlighted the difficulties that many mainstream pupils face.

Many mainstream pupils could benefit from a scheme of this kind. We know it and so do they. The national curriculum does not offer these pupils a broad and balanced curriculum either. There is little point in any pupil doing ten GCSEs with all the pressure and workload this entails. For a pupil who may struggle to achieve those E and F grades at GCSE, there is little point in doing seven GCSEs, and yet there is virtually no alternative. The authorities then wonder why truancy levels and exclusions are so high in secondary schools. The education system in Britain is robbing children of their childhood. The pressure of coursework, practicals and revision in Y11 is phenomenal. The expression about school being the happiest time of your life will not be in existence for very much longer. I would certainly not like to be 15 years old again because of the way our education system operates today. A note was left in The Resource after a particularly busy lunchtime. It simply read, 'I have a communication difficulty, can I be in The Resource?' Some of these children are brilliant pupils at Y9 and Y10. They work hard and give lessons all that they have. Their effort and determination has to be admired. However, in Y11, with the pressure of work and lack of time, it is not surprising that some pupils become disillusioned with the education system. Their motivation to succeed may decline. The system can offer few alternatives to them. We rightly celebrate the 50 per cent of pupils in an academically able school who achieve the magical five A–C grades at GCSE; for the other 50 per cent I worry.

The long vacation that schools enjoy in the summer can be a real bonus. However, for some pupils in The Resource it can be a time of stress and anxiety because home life cannot be as structured as school (nor should it be). Holidays away from the home can cause additional anxiety. In terms of work placements, six weeks off from school needs to be viewed as an opportunity. With the success of Integration into Work and the local publicity it has received, our confidence has increased and we will try anything that might benefit our pupils. In the first summer of the new millennium, one of our Y11 pupils wanted to get some paid work in the summer vacation. Staff and parents supported him in writing a letter of application and curriculum vitae. These were posted to about five different employers. A large store in Sheffield town centre wrote back inviting this pupil to an interview. A member of staff accompanied him on the morning of the interview. He was rewarded with three weeks of paid work in their offices. A member of staff supported the pupil on his first day in work and was very pleased with the attitude and guidance which the employer and employees appeared to be offering. This was a further experience for our pupil and he received a lovely thank you letter for his hard work. He could also buy his own tickets to see his favourite Sheffield football team for a while.

During the same summer vacation, one of our post-16 students had a two-week placement at HSBC bank. HSBC reported that he was the best work experience student they had ever had. Anthony, a Y10 pupil, worked with the IT technician at school for two weeks of the summer vacation and was paid.

Difficulties still remain, and always will because of individual need. In addition to the pupil who would like to work with animals, we have a boy who would love to work in a car showroom. He knows everything there is to know about cars and would make a superb salesperson. Our job is to search for a suitable employer. That search could take some time, or we could be lucky with the first letter and information pack sent out.

Integration into Work is a new structure that we have initiated. It is part of the solution and foundation for access and inclusion in later life. It will only be a success if the massive unemployment rate among adults with ASD is dramatically lowered from the un-acceptable levels of today. If Andrew is only an isolated example of what can be achieved, then we will have failed. Some of the challenges have been met through our Integration into Work scheme, but many still lie ahead.

# 7

# Our Charity
## The Chase for Cash

After an initial set-up grant from Sheffield LEA of £1000, we received no further money through official channels for the next four years. The £1000 was spent on chairs, tables, blinds and technological breakthroughs such as paper and coloured pencils. No money was allowed for IT equipment, not that £1000 would have gone very far. Nobody complained too much. The arguments were put forward in a rational and coherent way. No victories were really expected because this was the education sector.

The management of the school rightly argued that because our pupils spent most of their timetable in mainstream lessons, it would not be appropriate to give The Resource an annual allocation of funds. The headteacher argued that money given to The Resource would have to be taken from other departments within the school. This was at the time of a headteacher who was new to the school and only beginning on his learning curve about autism. The financial dilemma was that Sheffield LEA argued that there would be no further money available from them. Officers felt that the school should support The Resource with an annual allocation of funds. We sat in the middle of this debate, agreeing with both the LEA and the school. We could not disagree with the arguments that either party was putting forward. This situation must be mirrored many times in educational establishments across the country. We had a beautiful resource base and a growing pupil number and staff to match. We were faced with a group of people in the school who needed time and explanations to be able to accept that we were dedicated to changing the lives of our pupils for the better. What we did not have was money to purchase things the pupils needed in order to access the curriculum and life more fully. So much of society appears closed to people with autism. Five years of good quality access and integration would not begin to address the difficulties of people with autism and those without autism.

There were many items that we needed to purchase. It is never a comfortable feeling for any organisation (or individual) to realise that they have no funds. The most simple of pleasures can become fraught with difficulties. I found myself looking at pairs of scissors and reams of A4 paper in classrooms with something approaching envy. Storerooms and the central office in school were like an Aladdin's cave to me. Most projects in schools carry a cost, even if it is in terms of staff time. For The Resource, staff had the time, but no money to carry out their ideas. A computer was desperately needed. We had room for three computers with beautiful worktops that had been carefully measured to be the right working height for pupils to operate IT equipment. We did not have the money to buy the polish needed to keep these new worktops looking clean. We worked in a school that had whole rooms set up with computers. Pupils needed to work on their IT skills back in The Resource base. Most children with a severe communication disorder enjoy working at a computer. It can be a strength area. Computers do not have bad moods on a Friday afternoon and they do not shout at you.

With a naivety that can only be bred from sheer desperation, we began to write begging letters to large companies, accompanied by information about our work and plans. Our promotional leaflets at that time were equally naive and poorly produced. At that time, I knew the direction in which The Resource had to go, and I remember being upset when other people, people who had money to give away, did not seem to share our dreams. There must be hundreds of people who raise money for good causes who know and understand this feeling. I took the rejection letters personally. How could people fail to see and believe in what we were trying to do? The polite letters full of sympathy and good wishes for the future, but no cheque, made me even angrier. I had not realised that locating sources of finance and then being able to write successful bids was a whole new area of work. There are such people as professional fundraisers. This was another world to me. I spoke to some fundraisers who would take 25 per cent of any money they raised. One fundraiser wanted £1000 before he would begin work. My trust in these people was limited, and yet we were amateurs when it came to locating and accessing charitable funds.

Several months went by. Then that wonderful white envelope arrived from British Telecom, one of the companies we had written to. This time it was not a bill. Opening this envelope to find a cheque was a key moment. This cheque represented something concrete that proved we had reached somebody with our words and plans. A person in an office, whom I had never met, had read our literature and thought, 'Yes, that's a good idea'. The elation of holding that cheque for £1500 and realising that I could order a state-of-the-art computer monitor and printer will never be forgotten. The smile on my face lasted all week. We have received larger cheques than this in the last seven years. But this was the first and in many ways the most important. The thank you letter was dispatched by return post. Presentation packs of information were improved. The promotional leaflet became a little more 'polished'. We bought the best and most advanced computer in the school. Mainstream pupils and sixth formers came into The Resource at lunchtime just to stand and look at the machine. Andrew and Shaun, our first two pupils, invited their friends to come and play computer games on the new machine. Photographs were taken of children working at our computer. Exciting times!

However, difficulties with the projects we had chosen to carry out, especially the Integration Into Work scheme, were becoming only too apparent. Sainsbury's was only too happy to push me (kicking and screaming) through the door when Andrew, the pupil with whom I was shelf stacking, no longer needed my presence. However, some pupils who had placements on the Integration into Work scheme needed a higher level of support than Andrew. Individual pupils were requiring a year's worth of support in total. This did not lessen the importance of those placements, because each one became a vital part of the pupil's weekly curriculum. Some employers needed more support than others. If we reduced the support level for a pupil, we ran the risk of losing the placement. We learnt that employers are just the same as mainstream teachers. They have different levels of confidence and require a variety of support strategies.

The difficulty was that Integration into Work began to take increasing amounts of staff time. This carried the potential risk of having a detrimental effect on the work within school. The levels of support staff were offering to pupils, especially those who were new to the school, were stretched enough as it was. The success of Integration into Work in terms of improvements in self-esteem alone was enough to ensure that the scheme was never under threat. The truth was quite the contrary. Staff, pupils and their parents needed the scheme to expand. As increasing numbers of pupils progressed through school, the scheme needed more employers so we could offer a variety of opportunities to try to match their individual wishes. Money was needed to enable us to employ an extra member of staff. This member of staff was needed to ensure the continued expansion of the Integration into Work scheme. Cheques for £1500 would help, but would never be enough. Given the necessary finance, the issue of who would be the employer of this additional person also began to be of concern. The LEA was not approached to finance this idea. Experience had taught us that this was too far removed from their financial investment and role in education.

A further difficulty was the scenario of what would happen to our pupils after they left school at 16. The employment issues appeared only too clear (discussed in Chapter 6). Integration into Work could not stop suddenly for a student after the age of 16. Most of our pupils, along with their mainstream peers, would need to gain further qualifications after their final year at school. Access to employment depends to a large extent on further qualifications after the age of 16. It was felt that prospective employers must have no excuses when it came to offering paid work to young adults with autism in Sheffield.

Staff from The Resource began to visit Sheffield College. Our colleagues in the tertiary education system were brilliant. The additional needs department within the college was well organised and offered quality support which catered as far as possible to the individual needs of their students. Having commented in an earlier chapter that we do not like to enter the debating circle surrounding autism, it is felt that 'additional needs' is a much more appropriate term than 'special needs'. All children as individuals have special needs, and a smaller number have additional needs that require addressing.

Personnel at Sheffield College were also honest enough to recognise and suggest that the tertiary system was not prepared for our pupils at post-16; nor could they offer the expert support so vital to continued success and progress. The Integration into Work scheme would not be continued for some of our pupils as they progressed into Sheffield College, although they did have excellent links with a wide range of employers. The transition into the college system would be too much for most of our pupils to cope with. We could see five years of work being undone very quickly. Sheffield College is split on several different sites across the city. A potential 'watering down' of support was envisaged as one pupil would be placed on a course in one part of Sheffield, with another finding himself at a different site. Continuity of support and expertise would be lost. The idea of The Resource being the safe place of belonging and understanding would also disappear.

My gratitude to Sheffield College began when two of their managers began to look at this situation not as a problem, but as an opportunity. These two managers made the time and effort to visit The Resource and to meet staff and pupils. A partnership appeared to offer a possible way forward. We were asked to write a proposal to finance a feasibility study into the whole area of post-16 education for students with ASD in Sheffield. This took a lot of extra work and many tears as I struggled to write the study in the way managers within the college wanted it done. Learning a foreign language would probably have been easier. It is one of the most difficult 'bids' I had attempted up to this point. The first proposal was handed in on time and I waited for the verdict like a pupil waiting optimistically to see if he has an A or B grade. It is fair to say that had it been graded, it would have received an E. The two managers made some valid and positive suggestions about improvements and I returned home to try again.

The second attempt appeared to make everyone happy and the money was received (£10,000). The problem, or rather the deal, became crystal clear. Sheffield College would fund the salary cost for a person to run a post-16 provision, but we would have to find a suitable building for the base. This base needed to be at the school to aid transition and provide some continuity. In business terms, we were being offered a franchise deal by the college, and we had to make some kind of capital investment up-front to prove how serious a partner we would be.

A further difficulty was that King Ecgbert School was full and no space was available. The school had become oversubscribed and on several occasions I had caught the headteacher looking with envy at the space currently occupied by The Resource base. I did not feel it appropriate to ask him for a further room, as the sound of his laughter would have been upsetting. There was space to locate a new building as the school is surrounded by a lot of land, owned by Sheffield Council. We would need to raise in the region of £50,000 for some kind of building.

I began to fill in bid forms to every charitable organisation that existed and some that didn't. The response was dismal. The reason given 99 times out of 100 was that the bids were failing because The Resource was not a registered charity. The charitable organisations to which I was writing believed, because they had to believe it, that The Resource fell under the umbrella of Sheffield Education Department; therefore finance for our worthwhile projects should be easy to obtain. My first response to this was to write back and argue that this was nonsense. I wasted several months quietly (and sometimes noisily) fuming about the injustices of the whole rotten situation. It was as if we had run the marathon, only to be beaten by those runners with a sprint finish. I found a wonderful organisation within the council that could give me access to their database of charitable groups. I could not access this database because The Resource was not a registered charity. Then, with the encouragement of the whole team, plus a wife who continues to support me through good times and bad, I had to face reality.

If The Resource was failing to attract funding from external sources because it was not a registered charity, then let's get registered. As a teacher and a human being, I recognised that this was not the way things should be in the same way that the maths teacher realises that all is not well when he hands out textbooks that are 15 years old. A colleague did the hard work of registering The Resource as a charity. It takes several months to get everything organised. The legal work was carried out at no cost by some wonderful people in that profession. Very many faceless people from all walks of life have helped The Resource along the way. Every time this happens, it is a reminder that people are basically good and do want to help with projects that might improve opportunities for others. People within the Charity Commission were also very helpful and supportive. They provided us with several models we could use. Apart from the legal costs involved, it is inexpensive to become a charity. There is a small tax of 50 pence to acquire the authorised stamp of approval from the Commission.

The head of King Ecgbert's was understanding and approved of the move as long as the name of the school was incorporated into the title of the charity. Finally, some tired but willing parents foolishly said they would become trustees. It was felt that six trustees was about the right number. One parent was willing to stand as the chairperson, another the secretary and a third one as the treasurer. Parents are only too willing to work with professionals if they can see the benefits for their children. Strangely enough, the only people who questioned what we were doing were our managers in the Sheffield Education Department. It was one of the few occasions when a senior officer telephoned me at The Resource. There was not a lot that officers within the education department could do to stop us, but their questions about why we were becoming a charity did confuse me slightly. In fairness to them, what we wanted to achieve was so far beyond our normal role as educationists that it was perhaps too much for them to accept with good grace. Fortunately, the situation is very different today. Officers have become accustomed to staff in The Resource working in ways that challenge the accepted norms.

The cooperation we now receive from Sheffield LEA is much appreciated. What we have striven to do each step of the way is to build partnerships with organisations that want to be active and help. This is what the British government has encouraged professionals within education to do. Becoming a registered charity would enable The Resource to have access to many more partnerships.

We had a grand launch of our new charity with invited guests enjoying a lovely buffet lunch and wine. The local press were invited to see a cheque for £10,000 being handed over to us by a representative from a large British bank. A local ex-England football player was invited to accept the cheque on our behalf and pose for photographs. In the middle of these fifty or so guests were pupils and staff from The Resource. A short presentation was given and questions were invited from the audience. Almost inevitably one pupil from The Resource, DJ, put up his hand and asked if The Resource could now have a second computer and a pool table. The only possible response was 'yes'. We raised a further £1500 from this launch of the charity. The headteacher of the school very kindly paid the bill for lunch. Other people provided us with good leads, either in terms of finance or possible placements for the Integration into Work scheme. Most people at the launch represented companies from the private sector. It was a long way from what most people enter the education profession for; yet it had to be done if The Resource was going to attract the finance it needed.

Suddenly, life became a lot easier. We found a retired fundraiser who gave lots of free and valuable advice. He agreed to send me any bid forms he felt might be likely to offer The Resource some assistance. I became better at filling in bid forms. Raising finance from charitable sources is like having a second job. Time has to be found to carry out the job well. The council database for registered charities (called Fundfinder) became another valuable source of information. Being a registered charity, with that all-important charity number, opened the doors we had been knocking on for some time. Bids still failed, but lessons were learnt through rejection. A professional attitude was taken and rejections were no longer taken personally. A European bid was attempted, perhaps a little too early. The amount of work involved was immense. The subsequent failure taught us to stay a little closer to home in terms of the search for finance.

Trustees' meetings were held and this level of organisation has given much support, not only to me but also to the team of staff as a whole. The meetings gave me direct access to the views and opinions of parents. The support and encouragement I have received since the establishment of the charity in 1998 has been much appreciated. There is always somebody for me to turn to for guidance and support. Later on, trustees became a valuable source of 'parent power' when the future of The Resource came under threat.

The problems with Integration into Work being too successful were now more easily solved. The trustees and I felt it was important, in the spirit of charitable goodwill, to try to employ an additional member of staff through the New Deal. This is a government employment scheme only open to people who have had the misfortune to be unemployed for over six months. From a more realistic and selfish standpoint, the scheme offered some assistance with salary costs for the first three months and a generous training allowance. We had one applicant, and she appeared to be everything we were looking for. An interview panel was quickly formed consisting of the chair of trustees, myself and a support worker from The Resource. The appointment was made and our new employment support worker began a three-month trial period. She passed with flying colours, attended some training on autism and remained in post for two years. There is no question that we will always attempt to have at least one additional member of staff employed through the charity. In terms of the service we can offer to employers, our employment support worker is vital.

During the next 18 months, our employment support worker initiated and supported pupils on placements at a farm, Marks and Spencer, a local library and a nearby garden centre. She also visited pupils who already had placements and reported back on their progress. Our employment support worker completed the paperwork involved in the scheme, and this relieved me of a little pressure.

Obtaining the building we needed for a post-16 base no longer felt like walking through treacle, but more like a stroll in the park. Five bids were made to national charities. A further five bids went in to local Sheffield trust funds. The project had to be costed. A new double mobile classroom could be bought, transported and put on site for about £55,000. The furniture and IT equipment needed would add about another £1300. The regulations and paperwork involved are frightening. The council owned the land and so they wanted to charge ground rent – unbelievable yet true. The school would be offered the use of one of the classrooms in return for picking up the bill for heating, lighting and cleaning. This caused difficulties with the firm that organised the cleaning contract. A man had to come out to assess how long this new task would take in order to renegotiate the cleaning budget. New obstacles would appear on a weekly basis.

Two of the bids to national charities were successful. Four of the bids to local-based trust funds were successful. Some charities agree to finance a buildings project with very little fuss. For others, you have to jump through many hoops. It is always easier to attract finance for a capital project such as a building or piece of equipment. These one-off schemes appear easier for large charitable funds to contribute towards. Locating sources of funding for longer-term projects such as our employment support worker's salary is much more difficult. The council and their legal advisers decided to charge us the usual rate of ground rent and then pay it all back to us apart from 1p (or something like that). However, they made it crystal clear that they could throw us off their land if we had any wild parties in the mobile classroom. The deal seemed harsh, but we could cope with it.

Sheffield College was as good as its word. The person who had the daunting task of running our new post-16 provision was a support worker from The Resource. She is also the co-author of this book. The work at post-16 is discussed in more detail in Chapter 8. Our pupils would now continue to receive skilled support on their college courses. They could still return to their base at King Ecgbert School. Parents and trustees had got what they wanted. We had achieved something that still gives me a tremendous thrill every time I look out of the window at school – our very own building. To most visitors, it looks just like what it is, a double mobile classroom. It represents much more than this to staff and trustees. The mobile classroom stands as a working monument to what can be achieved with sheer determination and effort. Lots of people stood, waited and privately thought that it could not be done. When holes were dug for the foundations and the lorries rolled up with their heavy loads, pupils and staff alike watched through the windows of The Resource. The next bit of the puzzle was being put into place in front of our very eyes. The smiles were broad and long-lasting.

As already pointed out, raising the necessary finance to continue with our projects at post-16 and in employment is like having a second job. There are costs to this in terms of disruption to family life. One of the benefits is that it can lead you to meet groups of people you would otherwise not come into contact with. One such delightful collection of people was the women's fellowship group at a local Methodist church near school. This group of about 50 women invited me to talk to them at their church on a cold and windy night in January. It was a great evening, which they appeared to enjoy. Speaking in public does not come naturally and so I never look forward to nights such as this one. I had a great time listening to their stories about people with autism whom they knew either directly or indirectly. They adopted The Resource as their nominated charity for the year 2000. These local women held fashion shows, cake sales and coffee mornings. Later on that year, I was invited to their annual general meeting where they presented a cheque for £1650. It was a touching and heart-warming experience that I will never forget. I had the privilege of talking about autism and the work of The Resource to a group of local women who then worked very hard to raise money for us. Their next nominated charity is an organisation in Sheffield that works with people with schizophrenia. Life is a strange journey sometimes.

It could not get more strange than fifty mainstream pupils (and one lad from The Resource) with about ten teachers from school abseiling down the side of a ten-storey hotel in the city centre to raise money for The Resource. Christine Breakey and I also attempted the abseil and it was not pleasant. The money raised by these children and their teachers (£1800) just about made up for the pain and sheer terror. It is equally strange when people I do not know volunteer to run marathons and donate money to The Resource. Strange but wonderful.

Just when you think that life is good and things could not be going that much better, something inevitably comes along to spoil it all, and serves as a reminder that, in the public sector at least, making progress always involves a battle. Sadly, sometimes those battles have to be fought just to hold on to what has been achieved so far. It comes back to working in the public sector. The pressure on managers in local government to reduce what they see as costs must be immense. Managers and people in authority use the term 'savings'. The people who do the work can only see these savings as cuts in services. Ultimately, the end users are the losers.

By 1999, we had secured a staffing ratio in The Resource of 20 pupils, with eight staff. This ratio is adequate. Several of the support workers remained on temporary contracts, which is never ideal. The headteacher knew that at some point the budget for the staffing costs of The Resource would be delegated to his school budget. This was never an issue because it was inevitable that it would happen in line with current national legislation. Our relationship with the governors of the school was good. They had invited me to attend one of their meetings to discuss the work of The Resource. However, when the figures arrived showing how much money would be in the budget which the school would take over, it became clear that it was not enough to cover the salary costs of the eight staff. Staff in The Resource were despondent. Morale within many sectors of education is damaged enough as it is without others making the job even more difficult.

Several further meetings were arranged between officers from the LEA, the headteacher of the school and myself. Little further progress was made and the headteacher had no choice but to recommend that the governors refuse the delegated budget. It would never have been appropriate for the school to find several

thousand pounds from their own budget in order to help finance
The Resource. With hindsight, officers were never going to be
thrilled by this course of action. However, the school had little
choice and the headteacher had my full support. The responsibility weighed heavy on our shoulders. Several resources in
secondary schools in Sheffield that served pupils with special
needs had closed because of inadequate delegated budgets. It
appeared to be a kind of brinkmanship. These were nervous times
for all concerned, including the LEA officers, who were only
doing their job and trying to save a few thousand pounds of
public funds. The headteacher could not accept what would have
been a deficit budget. Making a member of staff redundant
would have been one option, but this, quite rightly, was never
discussed as a possibility.

The final twist, or sting in the tail, was a proposal by officers to
move the budget for The Resource to a special school in
Sheffield. Their headteacher and governors would become responsible for the finances and management of The Resource. This
caused uproar as any outsider could imagine. It really did feel like
a punishment for not 'playing the game'. The headteacher at
King Ecgbert School was livid. He did not want a group of staff
in his school being managed by the headteacher and governors of
another school. Trustees of our charity were equally horrified
that a special school could manage a mainstream inclusive
provision. This 'service' approach to pupils with severe communication disorders was ill-conceived and very badly managed.
One of my overriding concerns was that our supportive headteacher would finally hold up his hands in despair and close The
Resource. Headteachers are under immense pressure in our
schools and this was the last thing he needed. However, with his
experience and expertise, he handled the pressure far better than
I did. His calming influence at this time was much appreciated.

The headteacher of King Ecgbert arranged a series of
meetings with the director of education. Trustees also made ap-
pointments to see officers involved in this decision. Talking in

terms of battles may seem melodramatic to the reader. I can draw no other suitable parallels. This was the final struggle and there could be only one winner. Fortunately, and thanks to a director of education who did listen and accept that officers had made some mistakes, pupils at The Resource were the winners. The proposals for us to move to the special school were dropped. All employment contracts for the team of eight staff at The Resource ceased to be temporary. Whatever the staffing costs were from one year to the next would be met by the delegated budget. We could move on. However, the stress of these struggles must never be underestimated. My wife saw me shed too many tears during these difficult times. Too many excellent people within education have to struggle and battle to achieve the necessary resource levels for the benefit of our children. For many of these people, the inevitable cost is felt in terms of their health, pressure on their families and ultimately on their life expectancy. It should not have to be this way.

There are still times, usually filling in the next bid form having just had three polite refusals, when I question the whole picture. Inclusion, access, integration, education and employment issues should not be reliant on charity. They are too important and are too much of a human rights issue for that. However, I have had to accept, albeit grudgingly, that this is the way things are. We could have lost even more time being altruistic about the issues, but we would not have made as much progress. The ultimate consideration always has to be the needs of the pupils. If their needs dictate that some rules have to be broken and that political principles have to be put to one side, then so be it.

If systems will not change for the benefit of our children, we have to encourage them to do so. Making beneficial changes will usually involve financial and human investment. These changes for the better must be viewed as an investment and never a cost. In today's society, if this investment means a reliance on charity, it is up to people who raise this money to prove that the benefits are worthwhile. Once this is achieved, it will be time to knock on the door of Parliament to achieve state investment.

# 8

# Post-16

## The First Year

The background to the development of the partnership between King Ecgbert Integrated Resource Charity and The Sheffield College has been described in the previous chapter. This chapter takes a more personal view of the period immediately prior to the setting up of the post-16 provision, and the experiences of the first year. It also describes the lessons that were learnt, and how they have influenced further development of the provision.

**Background information.**

'By nature' (whatever that may mean!) I am a person who finds security in the knowledge that other people have done things first. I am not afraid of breaking new ground when it is required of me, but I see no sense in 'reinventing the wheel'. I am also quite a critical person. These things, when combined, help to make me a 'modifier'.

When I was appointed in August 1999, as support co-ordinator for students who have ASD at The Sheffield College, I thought that I would be able to modify what other people had done in a way which would suit the requirements of the new post-16 provision. I am an avid reader, so my first reaction was to read what other people had written about their experiences. The autobiographical works were both depressing and inspirational. They catalogued mistakes and misunderstandings, often made by the most well-intentioned, well-meaning and dedicated of teachers, but they also highlighted the significant difference which even one teacher who got it right could make to the life of someone who had autism. Even so, it seemed to me that people like Temple Grandin were really an exception and that most people who had ASD did not achieve in line with their potential. Those who did seemed to do this despite the system, which appeared to be acting against them. The more academic books, on the other hand, showed that very little had been written in this area. I found this quite incredible. Hugh Morgan (1996) expressed the view that 'the value of education for adults with learning disabilities has been demonstrated by many studies dating back to the early eighteenth century', but that despite this there was currently a 'paucity of literature available concerning the integration of adults with autism into the further education system within the UK'. He was right. There is very little.

Patricia Howlin (1997) suggested that this lack of available literature might be linked to the previous lack of inclusive and integrated opportunities for people who have ASD within secondary education, and subsequently further education colleges. Academic literature both influences and reflects current practice. On this occasion, I felt that it was lagging behind the practice. The picture that was presented was particularly negative and depressing. The literature suggested that further education for people who have autism was inadequate, both in terms of its availability and its approach, giving examples of a few successes, which I have to admit were lost on me at the time because of the impact of the failures and disasters which were described. I knew through my work at The Resource that there was a lack of integration and inclusion for people who have autism within schools and colleges. I don't think that I had entirely appreciated the full extent, or the impact which this had on those young people and their families, until this point. There were and still are students within further education colleges who have autism in many of its various forms, and many of these young people had and still have superb support which enables them to progress and achieve. There were and are many success stories. But the literature brought home to me the fact that these young people were probably just the tip of the iceberg. This was not the case for the vast majority of students who have an autistic spectrum disorder. Attitudes were changing, though, and some of the literature reflected that.

I was relieved to read of successful schemes, especially the Highfield House project in Nottingham and Oakfield House in Birmingham. I had been interested in the work of Whitegates Adult Services since meeting Fred Parsons in 1995 (see Chapter 4), so I was particularly interested in the Highfield House project, which is a working partnership between Whitegates and North Nottinghamshire College of Further Education (Morgan 1996). As well as meeting Fred Parsons, there were some staff from Whitegates on a course which I was attending. I had been very interested in their contribution to discussions and thought that The Resource shared views with them in terms of policy and approach. In addition, a small group of staff and parents from The Resource had visited Whitegates on some of The Resource development days. The feedback on the further education side had been very positive and had encouraged me to think that there might be parallels which could be drawn from that experience which would help the new post-16 provision.

I described myself at the beginning of this section as a critical person. In retrospect, I think that this isn't quite accurate. I enjoy critical analysis, particularly of the academic type, and tend to take a practical, critical approach to my work. I try to direct this in a positive and supportive way towards other people, but I don't know if I am always successful. The area where I am at my most ruthless is towards myself. I am particularly self-critical. I am also a talker.

During the period when the partnership with Sheffield College was secured, the staff team at The Resource was very strong. Autism as a subject is something which 'gets under your skin' and we spent a considerable amount of time, both in and out of school, talking about our work and reflecting on our practice.

In retrospect, this had its advantages. We were very critical and always thought that we should be doing things better than we were and we were constantly trying to work out approaches which accommodated autistic thinking and learning styles better. The result was that we became extremely creative.

Self-reflection and critical analysis also has its negative side, and it has to be said that we were our own biggest critics and our own worst enemies. Because we were always looking for ways to improve our practice, we didn't recognise that we were doing anything well. We were very hard on ourselves and there were times when we were quite negative and we had many low times.

By this time The Resource was receiving visitors from different parts of the country and we were getting a great deal of positive feedback and compliments about our work. We were amazed that people knew about us, and even more amazed that they were describing us as 'innovative', and 'ground breaking'. We still find this difficult to believe. As a group of people, we are not exceptional in any way and at times we feel extremely inadequate. During the six and a half years that I have worked at The Resource, I have never heard any of the staff professionally 'blow their own trumpet'. Personally, I feel that the continued progression and development of the provision hinges on the ability to be objectively critical and reflective about our work. If we ever thought that we knew all the answers and became complacent, I think we would cease to be effective.

### The approach at post-16

During the period immediately prior to my commencement at The Sheffield College, the Integrated Resource was described to me by a senior manager at the college as 'an integrated model that works'. She said, 'If it works in school, it will work in college. Why change it?' I found this comment particularly challenging and it caused me to re-evaluate the work of The Resource.

I had always seen The Resource as something that had evolved and not been created. I'm sure that in the very beginning there were theories and policies which someone, or a group of people, had put together, but essentially I saw The Resource as a dynamic entity, which was and still is continually evolving and changing. Because of this, I had not viewed it as a theoretical model and I was subjectively critical of it. Once I started to look at it objectively, though, I found that my opinions began to change.

Whether children who have autism should be educated in specialist schools or integrated into mainstream schools was and still is controversial. There are advantages and disadvantages to both. Generally, it is thought that specialist schools have a unique advantage because they have teachers who have the specialist knowledge and expertise which enables them to deal effectively with the difficulties associated with autism. They are also able to create the most suitable learning environment for those children to maximise their potential. In addition, they have a high staff: pupil ratio.

Patricia Howlin (1997) highlights the disadvantages of a special school education as limiting opportunities for social interaction and most importantly providing 'limited educational facilities'. Mainstream schools, in comparison, have teaching staff who are unlikely to have any knowledge of autism and a structure which is not 'autism friendly'. On the other hand, they can provide opportunities for social interaction and access to a wide curriculum.

When The Integrated Resource was set up, it aimed to combine the best of both. Unlike many specialist units attached to schools, the pupils in The Resource are fully integrated into mainstream classes. Staff who have autism-specific knowledge and skills provide in-class support, as well as specialist autism-specific tuition. They also provide the structured approach and 'autism friendly' environment which is necessary for our pupils. The staff: pupil ratio is set at 2.5 pupils to one member of staff, which is comparable with the special school sector.

When the Integrated Resource began in 1994, with two pupils in one mainstream class, no one envisaged that within five years we would be taking those same two pupils into a new autism-specific college provision. Yet, this was part of the process of change and evolution through which The Resource had moved. I had been viewing the post-16 provision as something new and different. Because of this, I had been searching for a new way of approaching things. I suddenly realised that the post-16 provision was not a new provision, but was a development or continuation of what was already provided at pre-16. I began to see that the senior manager was right. The Resource was and still is an 'integrated model that works'. The more I read about others' experiences, the more positive I felt about the work that we were doing in The Resource. I realised that we didn't have to start from scratch at post-16 and change everything. I also realised that I had searched enough and had found effective schemes which could be modified. The approach that the post-16 Resource would take would be based on the approach of the pre-16 Resource, while taking notice of the recommendations gleaned from other similar schemes and my reading.

### The practical reality

Prior to my interview and appointment, everything I had read identified the transition period from school to college as being an extremely difficult time for people who have ASD. Everything suggested that this would be greatly helped by the provision of a familiar person who could prepare the students, and so minimise the stress and remove as much uncertainty as possible. It also identified the importance of consistency of approach and staffing. I hoped that my appointment would achieve this, as I was already working at The Resource.

I am a committed Christian and I felt strongly in 1995, when I started work at The Resource, that I was 'meant' to be doing this type of work. I also felt that my professional background made me a suitable candidate for the position of post-16 Co-ordinator as I had previously taught at three local further education colleges, including The Sheffield College. I thought that the biggest advantage which I had at interview over the other candidates was that I could provide a link for the students, in terms of being a familiar person, between The Resource, and the College. There were some people who saw my appointment to the position of support co-ordinator as a foregone conclusion. I wasn't one of them! One of the most nerve-wracking days of my life was 16 June 1999. I don't know if the interviewing panel viewed my position in The Resource as an advantage, but I did get the job. I took up my appointment on 1st August 1999.

Whether working at The Resource was an advantage at the interview or not, it certainly was and still is an advantage in terms of doing the job. Very early on in the first year I attended a lecture at Hallam University, given by Nicola Martin, Head of Learning Support at the University of Derby. Nicola had been involved in a very similar project to ours and talked about her students' experiences in a further education college. She also highlighted the difficulties which students who have ASD experience during the transition from school to college. This can be a difficult time for all students, but is especially difficult for students who have ASD.

She also emphasised that, in addition to pupils' need for a familiar person, the break between finishing school and starting college was often a particularly stressful time for students who have ASD, because it is a period of nothingness. School is over and college has not yet started. This presents a real area of difficulty for people who have ASD, in terms of their identity. They are no longer school pupils, but they are not yet college students. We were able to minimise this difficulty for the two Year 11 students at The Resource because the transition period was viewed as a progression by everyone who was involved, especially by the students themselves.

Many secondary schools give their Year 11 pupils a study leave break prior to the commencement of the GCSE exams. Most Year 11 pupils are more than ready for this and look forward to it enthusiastically, greeting it in various stereotypically teenage ways. Typically, unlike the rest of the Year 11 pupils who do not have ASD, neither Shaun nor Andrew saw any reason to change their routine and participate in the study leave.

The study leave period is an extremely taxing time for the staff at The Resource as the daily structure and school timetable disappear completely. Resource staff have to provide a structured working day for four Year 11 pupils, as well as support the lower school pupils in their usual lessons and activities. Mainstream teachers can sometimes misguidedly view special needs teaching as a less skilled area of work than subject teaching, and there are many words spoken in jest which suggest that special needs is an easy option. Study leave is a time when these comments can be particularly galling for Resource staff, whose resources are stretched to their limits.

Despite that, the study leave time provided the perfect transition period for Shaun and Andrew – the two young people who were going to form the first year intake of the new autism specific, post-16 college provision. Both were sitting some GCSE examinations and consequently needed some structured revision sessions in The Resource, but this left plenty of time to provide a transition programme for them.

Again, I now realise in retrospect that this was an example of how The Resource has evolved to meet the needs of its students. Other people use the term 'needs-led' to describe the work at The Resource and talk about 'pre-access preparation'. We didn't use these labels at the time (nor do we use them now, for that matter). We just tried to listen to what our pupils were telling us they wanted and tried to give them what they needed.

### Pre-access preparation

For Shaun and Andrew, this started some time during their work experience placement in Year 9 (described in detail in Chapter 6). The Integration into Work scheme had been set up to equip Resource pupils with the skills and experience which would enable them to join the workplace alongside their neuro-typical peers. These work placements led quite naturally to vocational college courses.

Both Shaun and Andrew were fully involved in choosing their courses at college and applied through the usual route. Both filled in their own application forms with support from The Resource staff and their parents. As a result, they saw the progression to college as part of what they had been working towards since Year 9.

Shaun and Andrew were prepared for their interviews well in advance of the interview date. Over a number of teaching sessions, answers to possible questions were practised individually and then the interview situation was simulated as accurately as possible within a Resource classroom. Role-play is often used in The Resource as a teaching method, particularly to teach PSE and social skills, so both Shaun and Andrew were familiar with this method of teaching. They both enjoy watching their performance on video. In this way, we were able to practise the interview situation; view and evaluate it with them; involve them both in observing their own non-verbal communication skills; together identify areas which needed working on and teach new skills as required. We were also able to visit the college in advance, so that the environment was not totally alien to either of them. Both students were supported at interview, either by a member of staff from The Resource or by one of their parents. Both interviews went really well. Shaun's comment was that he thought that perhaps he was a little bit nervous, but that he had enjoyed it.

Once Shaun and Andrew had been accepted on the courses of their choice, it was possible to prepare them further for the start of their course. Andrew had been clear that he wanted to study Retail, in line with his work placement, which was at Sainsbury's. Shaun on the other hand was less certain of his direction, so chose to study on the Connections programme at the college. This programme is specifically designed to provide a core curriculum with a choice of vocational options, which enables students to gain credits and experiences that enable them to progress to a more specific course.

It was not possible for Shaun and Andrew to attend the same college centre, as Andrew's choice was restricted by the location of the Retail course and Shaun needed to be at a centre near his home to enable the development of independence. This meant that visits to two centres had to be organised. For ease of staffing, this meant that both students had to visit both centres. Again, in retrospect, we realise that this was a really useful thing to do. Shaun and Andrew had been together since they started primary school. They did not fit the conventional view of friends and it has to be said that, at times, they each found difficulty in the other's company. Because I do not have an autistic spectrum disorder, I had viewed their relationship in a purely neuro-typical way. They did not show their attachment for each other conventionally, so without thinking too much about it I had assumed that they weren't particularly attached to each other. This was very wrong. There is a very deep bond between them, felt most strongly by Shaun. He still feels the separation acutely. The joint visits helped him to adjust to the separation and gave him visible knowledge and awareness of where Andrew would be studying.

During the summer term of 1999, The Resource Charity had a mobile classroom installed in the grounds of King Ecgbert School. The intention was that Shaun and Andrew could attend King Ecgbert's in line with their individual needs and the needs of their courses. This enabled them both to maintain their links with The Resource and to meet up with each other. It also provided the progression link for them. Transition from school to college was not plagued by the difficulties I had read about. I think that this was due to the fact that it was more of a progression than a transition and, in some ways, the easiest part of the move to post-16.

## Sheffield College

The Sheffield College operates a policy of inclusion. Many people (myself included) find it difficult at first to understand the difference between inclusion and integration. Most people if asked will say that inclusion within education is to do with equal opportunities and students' rights of access to all courses, regardless of their disability. My current understanding of inclusion is that it is very much a practical issue, as well as an ideological one. Inclusion, within an educational setting, means finding the best match or fit between the individual student's learning requirement and the educational provision. Unlike integration, which means fitting the student into the provision, inclusion means devising or redesigning the learning environment to match the individual student's learning requirements. From this point of view, inclusion is not synonymous with integration, although the best learning environment for some students may well be an integrated one. Inclusion can also mean a mixture of integrated and discrete provision or even fully discrete provision if the student's learning requires it. This difference is particularly significant for people who have ASD, as their thinking and learning styles do not easily fit into conventional patterns. The nature of ASD requires individually designed learning packages which accommodate the associated uneven learning profiles and provide an autism-specific curriculum. This I believe is best accommodated within an inclusive framework.

The Sheffield College is one of the largest, if not the largest, further education college in the country, with five centres throughout the city. Each of the five centres is historically very individual and quite different. Each was a separate college before being amalgamated in 1989. All five buildings are also designed differently and each centre has its own distinctive culture and personality (if a college can have such a thing.) This means that inevitably some of the centres are more autism friendly than others. Many of the courses are taught in more than one centre, but Retail is only available at one centre. As I have already suggested, this meant that the choice of centre was restricted for Andrew. The Connections programme is taught throughout the college centres, but students are encouraged where possible to attend the centre nearest to their home. In line with the inclusive policy, it was possible to handpick which centre Shaun attended. At the time, I was not fully aware of the exact nature of the differences between each of the centres. The ability to work towards independent travel was very important for Shaun, so he attended the college centre which was most easily accessible from his home. Without knowing it at the time, this meant that Andrew and Shaun would have very different experiences of college life. It transpired that Andrew, who travelled on two buses to get to college, was attending the most autism friendly centre, while Shaun, who had less independent skills at the time, was travelling on a direct bus route but was attending the largest, busiest and least autism friendly centre in terms of its environment and culture. At that time, I was used to integrating people who have ASD into the systems which are available and had little knowledge of inclusion. It didn't really occur to me that we could mould and manipulate the system to suit our students. Had I been more aware of this at the time, things may have been quite different.

The main implication of Shaun's choice of centre was that in order successfully to manage his learning Shaun required an extremely high level of support throughout the whole of the year. This had its positive side. Shaun responded particularly well to the high level of one-to-one support which he received and has achieved far more than anyone expected of him, both academically and in the area of social skills and independence. From the provision's point of view, our experiences with Shaun provided a very steep learning curve. The lessons staff learned from Shaun about inclusion are now much more effectively applied.

Supporting across two centres would have been physically impossible if the Integrated Resource Charity had not provided extra part-time support in the form of the employment support worker, Jane Sommerville. Experience at The Resource had taught us that if we give our students a high level of support initially, we are able to establish patterns which our students will then prefer throughout their learning experience. We intended that both Shaun and Andrew would receive 100 per cent support for as long as it was required, but that independence would be a target for both of them.

Jane and I both found maintaining such a high level of one-to-one support to be physically and mentally exhausting. Our initial role was one of protection, as we had to anticipate how every situation would affect our students and remove all potential stress, by either preparing them in advance or avoiding the situation. This inevitably meant that we were taking all the stress on to ourselves, while trying to maintain a calm and professional exterior. We were often totally incoherent at the end of the day and found that we developed a directness in our communication which extended outside our workplace. This is a habit which I think I shall have for ever. (I am now totally incapable of 'small talk' and my family are amazed at how quickly I can extract information from new social contacts.) We realised that establishing good professional relationships with course tutors as quickly as possible was essential to the effectiveness of our role. What we didn't realise was just how much we would have to smile. This in itself was exhausting. There were times when we thought that we wouldn't be able to maintain our level of support, and we often worried about what the other would do if one of us became ill. Fortunately that never happened and we survived to tell the tale. We had the following structures in place, which I think helped us through that period.

1.  We had good communication with parents. At school, our preferred choice of communication had been a dictaphone. Both our students and their parents thought they had outgrown this means of communication so phone calls and notes home were frequent.

2.  Information was in place which gave lecturers brief outlines of the nature of the students' ASD; their areas of strengths; their areas of difficulty and tips and strategies for teaching.

3.  A timetable assumed paramount importance, even if it had to be rewritten at the end of each day, ready for the next.

4.  Rules were written and practised for lessons and social times.

5.  Good relationships with lecturers were fostered and their awareness of ASD was increased through the production of basic information booklets.

6.  Students' progress was continually assessed and discussed.

7.  Areas were targeted as suitable for independence and skills were taught to enable this.

8.  A consistent approach was considered essential.

9.  Time was set aside one day a week for reflection and rebuilding in The Integrated Resource.

Early on in the year, Jane and I noted that the physical environment was having a large effect on our students' ability to cope with their learning situation. We identified the following, which were more prevalent in one centre, as being particularly problematic:

1.  A noisy, crowded, busy, overheated environment could cause over-stimulation and excitement.

2.  Groups of students gathering at the entrances caused stress.

3.  Vending machines, because they often refused to accept coins.

4.  Cigarette smoking at the entrance to the building caused anxiety and stress.

5.  The bigger building with a split site limited independence.

6.  Moving around the college was both over-stimulating and stressful.

It was immediately apparent that even with an inclusion policy none of these were immediately within our control. Nevertheless, they still had to be addressed, in order to enable our students' inclusion. Some were more easily dealt with than others. For example, difficulties on entering the building because of people smoking outside can be easily altered by identifying an alternative entrance. Avoiding large groups of people could be dealt with in a similar way. In the longer term, policies could be changed which could alter the smoking areas. Some of the difficulties encountered in a split site were minimised through achieving access to the lift, and temperature control could be regulated by opening a window or advising more appropriate clothing. Even so, we were unable to address everything. For example, the vending machine still often refuses to accept coins and the college will always be large and busy. These matters necessitated teaching our students how to deal with them. Shaun is now able to approach one of the canteen staff for help if the vending machine in unpredictable. He has also learnt strategies which enable him to identify and manage any over-stimulation and excitement.

Jane and I also quickly realised that however well structured and well planned we were, college is inevitably an unpredictable place, especially at the beginning of the academic year. Rooms are sometimes double booked. Time tables change and lecturers are sometimes ill. This is particularly so on the larger courses which offer multiple options, such as Connections, and it is difficult to see how we could have managed it differently. I can only say that our support skills were stretched to their limits during the first three weeks of term. We have since thought that this could be avoided in future by opting out of the two-week induction period. This may work well for some of our students, but there could also be disadvantages, particularly in building relationships on behalf of our students with their peer group. This is still unresolved, but we are now much more aware of the need to 'hand pick' our courses and centres to match the needs of our students. In 2001 we provided transport across the city for one student to provide a better match of his needs with the centre.

Despite all the difficulties, Shaun thrived at college. He successfully completed his course and achieved 20 per cent independence during his first year. Andrew's experience was quite different. As I have already said, by pure chance Andrew attended the most autism friendly centre of the college. This meant that he experienced few of the difficulties identified above. In addition, the Retail course is a small, very tightly run course, taught by very experienced additional needs lecturers. As a result, Andrew successfully achieved an NVQ Level 1 in Retail by the end of the first year. He was also able to gain 80 per cent independence. Andrew's experience at college is covered in more detail in Chapter 9.

### Staff training

Our experience at post-16 highlighted the need for autism-specific staff training. Staff at The Resource are always requesting training in the field of autism. All too often, we are told that there is very little available. What there is tends to be more academic than practical. Jane and I had both been Resource trained. We had both attended courses at Hallam University on teaching students with autism and to a certain extent had also been self-taught in that we both devoured books written on the subject. We did not and still do not feel that we have been trained to do what we do.

The college environment is very different from the school environment. Pupils become students and are treated as young adults. They are expected to take their share of the responsibility for their own learning. As a result, control is much less of an issue than it is at school. Young people respond well to this and I have been amazed at how young people who were labelled as disruptive at school become responsible and mature in college. There is a downside to this when working with people who have ASD, which Hugh Morgan (1996) refers to as 'issues of normalisation'. People who have ASD have unconventional understanding and perceptions of the world around them which impact heavily on their ability to think abstractly and make choices for themselves. The college staff rightly seek to empower students who have disabilities and encourage them to make their own choices and decisions. This is extremely difficult and often stressful for people who need those choices to be based in concrete rather than abstract terms, in other words people who have ASD. Jane and I seemed extremely directive within this setting and sometimes felt that we had no alternative but to make choices on behalf of our students, because they didn't have a concrete framework within which to make those choices. We sometimes felt we were disapproved of or challenged because of this and we often needed to justify our actions and explain the reasons behind our approach.

In line with this, there is not as much need for rules and structure at college. Putting your hand up is no longer the appropriate method for catching your lecturer's attention, as it was in school. It had been difficult to teach our students how to take turns in conversation and how not to interrupt. Now, they were expected to do just that. This was extremely difficult and required formal teaching, as well as continuous on-the-job coaching and guidance. It continues to be a difficult area for our students and highlights the importance of increasing awareness of ASD and providing staff training for mainstream lecturers. Those lecturers whose understanding of ASD has increased through involvement with our students have learnt to pick up on these difficult areas of communication and help out our students at such times. It is also interesting to see how they apply their increased knowledge to other students in different groups.

The result of the increase in autism awareness was that it very quickly became apparent that there were other students within the college who staff thought might also have ASD, but had not been formally diagnosed. Once lecturers heard about the provision, we were inundated with queries and requests about other students. We were in danger of taking on more than we could effectively manage and we had to be quite strong to resist this. It was obvious that there was a need for some form of assessment, which could be used to identify students' needs and if necessary refer them for a formal assessment. There were other additional needs lecturers within the college who had skills and experience in working with students with autism. Jane and I were very privileged to be able to work with one of them – Ann Briggs. Together we produced an assessment package, which was designed for lecturers' use. This is now used to help identify students' needs and direct the existing support more effectively.

We found that one of the biggest difficulties we face when we start working with people who are new to ASD is that they invariably find it difficult to understand that ASD does not fit their perception of 'learning difficulties'. Alternatively, if they know anything about ASD, it tends to be a fixed stereotypical view of classic autism as portrayed by Dustin Hoffman in *Rainman*. In reality, few people who have autism fit this stereotype, but it is still the most well-known image. The typically uneven learning profile that students who have ASD show seems to present difficulties for most lecturers, especially in terms of accessing the curriculum and assessing students' learning. They also find it difficult to view ASD as primarily a communication difficulty, which is not necessarily accompanied by learning difficulties. They often bring with them preconceived ideas and attitudes, which may have worked well with other students, but are fatal when working with students who have ASD. Two examples of this are using humour to 'jolly people along' and touching students.

During the first year, this was particularly difficult for Shaun. Like most people who have ASD, Shaun does not always understand humour, innuendo, sarcasm and jokes. He is aware that he is expected to smile and laugh on occasions and will pick up on the cues from those around him in order to participate more fully. He can, however, get very excited by excessive use of these things. At these times, it is difficult for him to manage his own behaviour.

Supporting students in mainstream classes requires a huge amount of tact and diplomacy in order to maintain good working relationships under sometimes difficult circumstances. We don't always get it right, but we try to negotiate the best learning environment for our students, as tactfully as possible. We have found that approaching lecturers as professional equals earns us the most respect and the quickest action. Our first tactic is always to explain the student's learning style, within an autistic perspective, to the lecturer. Most lecturers want to do the best for their students and are more than willing to adapt their teaching methods in order to minimise the students' difficulties. This is often all that is required of us and a more appropriate teaching strategy is found and used. There was one occasion when this didn't work, however, and Jane and I had to find an alternative method of negotiation. This related to Shaun's excitability regarding the use of humour. On this occasion, we rewrote Shaun's personal profile in a way that emphasised his particular difficulties with this one area. It seemed to work and no offence was caused.

We have found that problems are less likely to arise if we can address students' lecturers and their peer group at the outset of the course. In this way, we can provide information on ASD, but most particularly we can provide information which is specific to each individual student. This was especially evidenced when we were asked to support a student who had recently been diagnosed as having Asperger's syndrome. The lack of diagnosis and the inevitable misunderstanding of his difficulties had led to an extremely difficult situation for this student. He was very stressed and as a result was showing obsessive and ritualistic behaviours, with the effect that he was unable to achieve academically.

For a variety of reasons, the decision was made to give the student a fresh start and to transfer him to a different learning centre to continue his studies. One hundred per cent specialist support was introduced for a very short period of time, in order to enable him to manage the change; after about two or three weeks this was reduced to 50 per cent. This was very successful for the student and we saw an almost immediate reduction of his stress levels and autistic behaviours. He is hoping to progress to university later this year. The provision of specialist support unquestionably played a part in this achievement, but the biggest influence was the partnership forged between the specialist support team and the subject lecturers. This enabled the subject lecturers to learn autism-specific skills, so that they could provide the most appropriate style of teaching and assessment for this student.

Staff training features in most of the literature on autism as a prerequisite to the successful inclusion of students who have ASD. The structured approach and visual methods used for our students could easily be used across the board and many students would benefit from this. Similarly, alternative forms of assessment to the written word would also benefit many other students. Autism-specific training for all teaching staff is probably an ideal which, given the limited resources and funding limitations, is unlikely to be attained. In the meantime, it is essential that all support staff who work in this area have autism-specific skills, which they can then use to inform others.

### Summary of lessons learnt

Four new students were to progress from The Resource to the post-16 provision in September 2000, more than tripling the initial number. The college agreed to provide two new learning support staff for the provision and I was keen that any lessons which Jane and I had learnt from the first year would influence further development. The end of the academic year provided a time for reflection and assessment, from which we made a number of personal recommendations:

*Transition*

This must be carefully planned, particularly for students who are new to us (by which I mean not from The Resource). Ideally, we should be involved from the transition review in Year 9, so that we can work with the student and develop the idea of progression rather than transition. This would enable the students to be better matched to the best course at the outset. Visits must be arranged to the relevant centres; where possible, students should meet their lecturers prior to the commencement of teaching and again, where possible, teaching rooms should be visited. Timetables should be given if they are available. Ideally, we would like to develop preparation packs for students to keep over the summer holidays (now developed for use in September 2001). These would include maps of the building, photographs of areas such as reception, toilets, canteen. etc. Photographs of staff would be appropriate, as well as a 'What to do if…' section. These would be individually made for each student in the most appropriate medium, for example, written, pictorial or a floppy disk.

*Links with home*

Parents and carers must feel confident in the support which their son or daughter is receiving. A good communication network must therefore be in place at the outset. Dictaphones should be provided and used if appropriate for this purpose.

*Support staff*

The support staff who work with students from The Post-16 Resource should have autism specific skills already in place, or, if this is not possible, must have the right personal characteristics, ability and approach which will enable them to learn quickly. Basic training should be provided before they commence work. A post-16 policy document should be in place by September 2001, which will help clarify and maintain a united approach and policy for supporting students.

## Lecturing staff

Lecturers must have the following information to help them when working with students who have ASD:

1. basic information and awareness of ASD: a booklet has been produced specifically for this

2. information specifically on how the individual student is affected by ASD. This would include a student profile and an explanation of the student's learning style and information on autistic thinking

3. teaching tips for working with the individual student. This would include areas such as the importance of structure; consistency of approach; the use of clear, unambiguous language and the use of visual forms of communication

4. lecturers should also have access to specialist support for advice.

## The student's peer group

Ideally, the student's peer group should be made aware of the nature of ASD, provided that this is acceptable to the student. This should be addressed within the tutorial period in a positive way and cover the following information:

- a simple explanation of ASD
- relevant information about how ASD affects the individual student
- tips on dealing with potentially difficult situations
- things to avoid (if necessary)
- an explanation of the role of the support worker within lessons
- a period for questions and answers.

### Progression and assessment

A planned programme of progression should be in place that sets reachable targets, which are additional to the usual lesson targets. This must be ongoing and assessed and evaluated regularly. New targets must be put in place continually to ensure that the student progresses.

### Levels of independence and support

These must be individually set, to ensure that each individual student receives the correct amount of support. This may involve 100 per cent support initially for some students and should be included in the progression and assessment programme discussed above. It should be continually assessed to achieve a maximum level of independence for each individual student.

### Curriculum

This may need to be continually renegotiated with subject tutors to ensure its appropriateness for the individual student who has ASD. This will require individual learning programmes for some students. The curriculum must also include time for autism-specific teaching to be timetabled.

### Assessment

Autism-specific forms of assessment, which accommodate autistic thinking and learning styles, should be produced wherever appropriate. There may also be a need to negotiate alternative methods of moderation and accreditation.

### Work placements

These need to be carefully identified and negotiated on an individual basis for students who have ASD. Specific information should be provided for the placement supervisor, which covers the same areas as the information provided for lecturers. Specialist support should be provided in the workplace, together with a planned programme of independence.

## The present and future

At present, there are seven students in the autism-specific, post-16 provision. All have one-to-one support, but the amount of support each student has varies considerably according to the individual. It is sometimes suggested that The Resource and the post-16 provision only take the more able end of the spectrum, or that all of our students have Asperger's syndrome. This is neither true, nor is it helpful to make such distinctions. We cater for a wide range of students across the autistic spectrum. All of our students at present use spoken language, at varying levels of skill and sophistication. Entrance criteria and decisions are not based on degree or severity of autism as it would in fact be virtually impossible and undesirable to do this. Asperger's syndrome is not, as is often said, 'a milder form of autism'. It is perhaps more subtle, but this in itself brings its own difficulties.

In practice, students who are diagnosed as having Asperger's syndrome may need higher levels of support for a number of reasons, but more noticeably because they are often studying higher level courses, which require higher level communication skills, particularly in the area of organisation. It is suggested that one of the differences between Asperger's syndrome and autism may be that people who have Asperger's syndrome are more socially aware than people who have autism and their need for social contact is greater. This understandably increases the risk of rejection and failure. When viewed in this light, it can be seen that people who have Asperger's syndrome require considerable support and autism-specific teaching in the area of social skills and personal relationships. Asperger's syndrome is not mild by any standard. At present we have students who are successfully achieving on the following courses:

- Advanced GNVQ Computing

- City and Guilds Computing
- NVQ Level 1 Retail
- NVQ Level 2 Retail
- Connections – a foundation programme
- NVQ Level 1 Bakery
- NVQ Level 1 in Business and Office Administration.

The potential for growth is enormous. We are on-line to double our student numbers next year. This will include accessing the following courses in addition to the ones already mentioned:

- Electrical Engineering
- Access Level Computing
- Vehicle Maintenance.

The worrying thing is that this is probably only the tip of the iceberg. We have become increasingly aware that there are many more young people who would benefit from being part of the post-16 provision. It is tempting to try to accommodate all of them. This, however, could be counterproductive as it would spread our limited resources thinly, making us eventually ineffective. This is a problem for management and I'm sure they are aware of it. My own view is that autism is very firmly on the agenda at Sheffield College. Awareness has been and continues to be raised. Staff are asking for more information and training in autism-specific skills. This can only benefit the service and contribute to its improvement. The future has to be better than the past.

# 9

# Andrew's Story

Andrew was one of the first pupils to begin his secondary education in The Resource at King Ecgbert School in September 1994. He has taught us much and rewarded us even more. Andrew and the other pupil who entered The Resource were our guinea pigs. They were also our pioneers. They taught us what works well in terms of integration and inclusion and what there is little point in pursuing as worthwhile and meaningful goals. Andrew continues to do this in his post-16 education and in paid employment.

Andrew made friends in his form because of his fun-loving nature and knowledge of things such as the latest *Star Wars* film, which things gave him some street credibility among his peers. He came to us from a small special primary school. The stress of transition for him and all our pupils is immense. The level of anxiety Andrew felt in his first few weeks in a busy mainstream secondary school can only be guessed at. Adults with autism talk of their anxiety levels as something that non-autistic people cannot comprehend easily. I have every reason to believe this. Secondary schools at their worst can be extremely hostile places for children. The narrow corridors at King Ecgbert that were designed for a school of 800 pupils now have to cope with numbers of well over a thousand. The acoustics in the gymnasiums are horrendous and they make listening to verbal instructions almost impossible. Male changing rooms are still places where bigger boys take things from smaller ones. They are loud, smelly and frightening places. There were many times when I questioned whether we had any right to expect Andrew and Shaun to be able to cope in this environment.

However, the preparation that Andrew needed before he began his time at The Resource was well planned and thorough. He visited the school on six separate occasions before the official start of term. The first two visits were spent walking around the buildings with map in hand. The following visits were used to experience the busy movement of changeover time, sit in on some lessons, and have dinner in the school canteen. Mainstream staff were introduced to Andrew and his friend. Their confidence grew with each visit.

This preparation meant that on the Y6 open day in July, when 180 mainstream pupils came to their new secondary school for the whole day, Andrew felt comfortable and already knew many of the 'answers'. Integration at its best is dependent on providing every conceivable advantage we can give to our pupils. Andrew also began to do nasty things such as homework in his final term at the primary special school. His primary teacher was given the first half-term's work of Year 7 in the French curriculum. The advantage was offered and taken – nothing magical, just common-sense stuff and the more of it, the better.

Andrew settled into his timetable with great ease. There are so many factors in secondary education that can work to the advantage of pupils with severe communication disorders. There are written timetables, definite start and stop times to lessons and bells that ring to signify this (although the loud noise of bells takes a while to get accustomed to). The fact that pupils know which teacher they have next gives added security to children such as Andrew. Teachers who are absent through illness have their names put on a list together with the name of the teacher who will cover their lesson, so we could forewarn our pupils. The number of nice surprises that occur in lessons is minimal, and it is rare (except in drama and music) for any group work to be attempted. With this security and predictability, Andrew not only knew his timetable by the end of the second week, but mine as well. One of the factors that makes some of our pupils stand out in lessons is that, despite knowing their timetable and everybody else's backwards, the piece of paper on which it is written may still come out of the bag and be placed on the table for every lesson. It is a visual 'comfort blanket'.

Andrew and the other pupil (who were both in the same form) received full support for the first term. This 'front-weighted' support is vital if integration is to stand any chance of success. The support included assistance with crossing the road, because of the split site nature of the school, support at dinner and break times, and waiting for the council transport at the end of school. The other advantage was that my co-worker and I got to know the other 28 mainstream pupils in the form quite well. The hope was that they would be able to witness at first hand on a daily basis how we related to Andrew. As a group of 11-year-olds, those pupils were told about Andrew's autism, what it might mean for him, what their role was (if they chose to have one) and given time to ask questions. They were brilliant. In difficult lessons such as PE, I never witnessed Andrew being excluded. These children benefited from having Andrew and Shaun in their form. They also benefited from having a high level of support from people they came to trust and like.

After the first term, Andrew needed to spend more time in The Resource working on communication and life skills. Geography was dropped, which gave us and Andrew two further hours a week in The Resource. This was in addition to the one lesson we had insisted on from the start (RE is not attempted and we obtain written permission from parents to allow this). With some work on road safety and risk taking, Andrew became independent in crossing the road between buildings. He worked through our introductory teaching package which, as well as on road safety, includes simple lessons on registration, calling a male teacher 'Sir' and a female teacher 'Miss' and teacher recognition (using photographs). This use of photographs to enable name learning got to the point where one of our pupils would ask visitors to The Resource to stand still and have their picture taken.

Some basic assessments were carried out with Andrew on the social use of language and self-image. These gave us an idea of what Andrew thought about himself. They also gave us opportunities to find out what Andrew liked to do, as well as the things he was not so keen on. Role-play was used to explore potentially difficult social situations and Andrew was assessed on how he managed in them. An example might be to pretend that he was playing football with friends and the ball is kicked into a neighbour's garden. Andrew had to talk to the neighbour (played by a member of staff), explain the situation and perhaps retrieve the ball. With more complex social situations, Andrew became increasingly unsure and upset.

Andrew also had life skill lessons in The Resource. The road safety lessons were written on the advice of a local police expert. Andrew became very cautious when crossing the road and this was just what we wanted. The message clearly given was that if any cars were moving, it was not safe to cross.

Andrew had great difficulties in learning to use the telephone. Lots of role-play was used and conversations were practised repeatedly. We decided that he would telephone his mother to ask what was for tea. It proved a tense and stressful activity for Andrew to complete. Several weeks of trying to carry out the task brought frustration and tears. The pressure was intense because his friend had completed all the tasks using the telephone with relative ease. Eventually, Andrew did phone his mother and had the planned conversation. When he came off the phone, he proudly announced that this was the first time he had ever phoned anyone. Andrew had forgotten to tell me before that this was the case. Nothing ever seemed as difficult again after this. Andrew appeared to appreciate that I had been patient and always calm. He gained my complete admiration for completing a task that was one of the most difficult things he had ever attempted.

Learning to use public transport was important to Andrew. He wanted the benefits of independent travel. He accomplished this quickly and began to come to school using public transport. The homeward journey was more difficult and we retained the council-provided transport for this.

He also had PSE lessons that focused on friendship at Key Stage 3. When he was an older pupil, Andrew had lessons on puberty, change and development. These were at a pace and content that suited his needs. Andrew became very angry and upset if certain key words were mentioned. We never understood the whys and wherefores of this. The problem was that other pupils (including some from The Resource) realised that they could whisper these key words to Andrew and then sit back and 'watch the show'. It took several years of discussion with Andrew to develop strategies that he could apply to keep himself calm. One of the messages clearly given has to be for the pupil to remain calm, and then seek assistance. Being told to 'ignore it' will not usually work without more detailed explanations.

With the foundations built in term one, Andrew slowly began to gain some independent lessons in terms two and three of his first year. Maths is a subject that is reorganised along ability lines quite early in most secondary schools. The setting of children in key areas such as maths was of great help to Andrew. The pace of lessons in his new maths set was much more appropriate to Andrew's needs, and the number of pupils in lower sets is remarkably small (there were 18 children in his maths set). This became one area in which Andrew could gain some independence. In other areas that were more dependent on literacy skills, Andrew found lessons more difficult. Fortunately, he had English in a smaller group that focused on literacy skills, and so he could gain a little independence in that subject. History was one lesson where Andrew could gain some independence. A wonderful teacher made this easier. Once I was sure Andrew could work independently and knew what to do next, I went to sit in the teacher's office where I could be called if needed.

A lot has been written about the possible effects on main-stream pupils of integrating pupils with additional needs. Some adults with autism or Asperger's syndrome have not had happy experiences within mainstream schools. Our experiences only extend over seven years. Undoubtedly, integration must be about serving the needs of mainstream pupils as well. They can make or break any attempts involving integration and inclusion. The first form of pupils we worked with were our 'guinea pigs', just as much as Andrew and his friend. They encouraged us to be ordinary human beings as well as teachers. They wanted adults who could not only explain about ASD, but who could also have a laugh and joke when appropriate. We were blessed with a superb group of children. One of these pupils (now an A-level student at the school) wrote down some of her thoughts regarding Andrew, his friend Shaun and staff from The Resource:

> When Shaun and Andrew were put in our form, the first thing I remember was this big, tall man with shoulder length hair and a bright green jacket standing in front of us. We were all new to the school and so sat, quaking in our boots while Mr Matthew introduced himself. He explained that he would be seeing a lot more of us, as he would be supporting Shaun and Andrew. Throughout the next five years, Shaun, Andrew, and the rest of our form received constant support from Resource staff who accompanied the boys in their lessons.
>
> At times it was difficult for the rest of the form. One of the children might become angry and shout or swear. No-body appeared to do anything. But, as we grew up we learnt that Shaun couldn't always help getting angry, and Andrew couldn't always help getting wound up by the smallest of things. But, I think lessons in our form were al-ways so much more interesting than those of other forms. No other form ever had chisels flying across the work-shop or the contagious fits of giggles during lessons, as our class did. Shaun was the louder of the two and often

came out with remarks that would have us all in fits for the next hour. One that sticks in my mind was his referral to a cover teacher (since left the school) as a 'boring, middle-aged barbarian'. Needless to say, the class got very little work done that lesson. Teachers were good with Shaun and Andrew. Most seemed to have got the balance right of excusing minor incidents, but making sure they acted in authority in more serious cases of misdemeanour.

Having Shaun and Andrew in our class meant that we had the benefit of extra support when and where we needed it. Matthew in particular became a firm friend with members of the form and a group of us used to spend lunchtimes in The Resource with Mr Matthew and the boys. For Shaun and Andrew, I would like to think that being in a class such as ours was of great benefit to them. I think the best thing that could have happened to them was to have been placed in a mainstream school. At King Ecgbert, they learned about dealing with people, others with learning difficulties as well as those without. They learnt to deal with teachers, dinner staff, administrative staff and also to handle themselves: things such as their own lunch money and homework, etc.

For myself and the rest of the class, there was the benefit of extra support, but also the benefit of learning to deal with people who have learning or communication difficulties. We learned to understand the misunderstood; why they had outbursts of anger or shouted at teachers. But, the most valuable thing I gained was a friendship. I became good friends with Shaun, and shed a tear on the last day of school when we said goodbye. He gave me a hug and then signed my school sweatshirt 'with luv Shaun XXX'.

There were difficult times and I'd be lying if I said there weren't, but I don't remember them. The good times easily outweighed them. Our class was a special form.

> Shaun and Andrew, and the relationship that we all had as
> a form made us just that.

Andrew was the first pupil who entered the Integration into
Work scheme (see Chapter 6). He progressed well over the three
years of his placement with Sainsbury's. He learned about
stacking fruit and vegetables. However, the vegetable section of
the store was very close to the video department. It took a while
for Andrew to realise that he could not stand and watch the latest
video releases playing on a nearby TV screen. Andrew wanted to
help with packing customers' bags at the checkout tills.
Sainsbury's were brilliant about this, but did require a member of
staff from The Resource to assist for the first couple of mornings.
Andrew had little difficulty in learning how to catch the bus back
to school after he had enjoyed lunch in the staff canteen. He
received a wonderful reference from his manager at the store.

Integration into Work certainly worked for Andrew. He had
the placement for one morning a week for three years. For the
vast majority of this time, Andrew was independent. However,
from time to time, difficulties will arise and advice needs to be
offered to the employer. Usually this is carried this out by staff
from The Resource. In times of apparent crisis, if the support is
not available quickly there could be real problems. Sometimes
there is an element of luck involved. Andrew's mother was doing
her shopping at the store one morning when he was on
placement. Some of the staff at the store got to know Andrew's
mother. On this particular morning, she was told that Andrew
was in the staff toilets in floods of tears. She was allowed 'back-
stage' to the staff toilets and asked Andrew (through the closed
toilet door) what had happened. Andrew recounted a tale of
helping an elderly lady to pack her bags. This lady had two
trolleys full of shopping and so Andrew had helped to push one
of them to the lady's car. At the car, he had loaded the bags into
the boot. This wonderful lady was clearly grateful for the service
that Andrew had delivered. As her way of thanking Andrew, she
uttered the fatal line, 'You've been so helpful, I could take you

home with me'. Andrew was mortified because he did not want to go to this lady's house, and so ran back into the store wailing loudly. This incident underlined the fact that we had to make it clearer to employers that they must telephone us in the event of any difficulties.

Andrew did not have the necessary range of cognitive skills to enable him to take a large number of GCSEs. It would have been a waste of his time and ours. What he did do at Key Stage 4 was to begin work on an National Vocational Qualification (NVQ) in Retail. Our newly emerging link with Sheffield College began to have direct benefits, as a member of our staff could become skilled in delivering the units of learning involved. Andrew could apply the knowledge from his work placement at Sainsbury's directly to tasks he was learning about in The Resource. Andrew, supported by the member of staff, began to build a portfolio of work that was required for a post-16 course. He completed two of the six units before leaving The Resource to continue his education at college. Andrew began the NVQ in Retail at college already having a good basis of knowledge. This idea of offering every conceivable advantage brings success at many different levels. Andrew could focus on settling into the routines of college life without having to worry about the content of his course.

This process was continued at post-16, with the added benefit of some paid work with Sainsbury's. In his first term at college, Andrew was offered an interview at Sainsbury's. It was coming up to the Christmas period when supermarkets take on extra staff on a temporary basis. Sainsbury's insisted (quite rightly) that Andrew could not be supported in the interview situation. We did what most people would have done and panicked. Interviews are not pleasant, despite the fact that we knew the personnel manager at the store would be very kind and friendly. Preparation became the key. Andrew was recorded on video in The Resource in an interview situation. Every conceivable question was discussed with Andrew and his responses were 'polished'. Body language was examined in detail and Andrew came up with his most favoured sitting position. Leaning back on his chair with his arm casually draped over the back was not allowed. Videos were made and shown to Andrew. He found the process both fun and a little embarrassing. It is not always easy to hear your own voice and see yourself as others see you. However, it gave Andrew an insight into the whole process of interviews and together we made one or two minor alterations to his answers. Making it clear to Andrew that he could not swear, even in this pressurised situation of direct questioning, was one of the minor alterations we discussed. Basic rules of eye contact were reiterated with Andrew.

The big day came and a colleague waited outside the interview room at Sainsbury's. I'm not sure who was the more nervous. Lengthy discussions had occurred between staff in The Resource about Andrew wearing a tie, and whether this should be tucked in or out of his trousers. We need not have worried. Andrew was rewarded with a four-hour shift on Fridays. This would fit in beautifully with his college course. He was delighted and we had a party. After the Christmas period, the store laid off several of the temporary workers. Andrew's services were retained. Before we could breathe a sigh of relief, Sainsbury's offered Andrew a further four-hour shift on Saturdays. The hours would be from 9am to 1pm. This gave Andrew a real problem because he enjoys watching Saturday morning TV. It is part of his ritual, and besides, Andrew does not see Saturday as a working day. Unfortunately, it was a difficult choice for Andrew as the store was altering all staff contracts. He either worked on a Saturday or lost his Friday shift as well. In discussion with Andrew, he grudgingly accepted that if Sainsbury's would permit him to work a later shift on Saturdays, he would give it a try. The personnel manager was phoned and this proposition was put to her with bated breath. We were thankful that she agreed to our proposal with no hesitation. We are deeply indebted to Sainsbury's.

Andrew's and Shaun's move to post-16 was in retrospect a major chapter in the life of The Resource. They were paving the way for the other 15 Resource pupils and were excellent role models. Chapter 8 has described how the decision was made which resulted in Andrew attending what turned out to be the most autism friendly of The Sheffield College centres. The Loxley centre is in quite a rural location, with lots of space around it. It is light and airy and has a very relaxed and friendly atmosphere. We didn't realise at the time just how beneficial this would be for Andrew. I waited in the foyer for Andrew and his mother to arrive on the first morning of term, and I don't know which of us was the most nervous. I think it was me! Andrew later paid me a huge compliment and said that he was feeling nervous until he saw me. My nervousness continued for a little while longer than his, but quickly disappeared once I met the Retail staff.

The Retail course is a mainstream course that has the advantage of being taught by extremely skilled and knowledgeable additional needs lecturers. The big advantage of this for us was that they very quickly understood the nature of autism and were able to recognise and address Andrew's autistic thinking and learning style. This meant that Andrew's needs were accommodated from the very beginning, and once he began to feel settled it was possible to introduce independence for him in some areas. Throughout the year this was gradually increased. There were some areas of the curriculum which have always remained difficult for Andrew. He continues to have support in English, and anything which involves a high level of group activity is also difficult for him, but he continues to make progress and is quite a model of success.

The students from the Retail course run a small shop within the college. Andrew took his turn with the other students from his group in working in the Loxshop. He was able to practise many skills that have been invaluable to him in his work placement. Towards the end of the year, I interviewed Andrew to try to find out his feelings about his experience at college. This was particularly interesting and enlightening for me. I think that including the pictures he drew for the interview and the interview transcript at this point are a good way of letting Andrew speak for himself.

Andrew likes drawing, so I asked him to draw faces that demonstrated a range of feelings which I wanted to include in my interview with him. As he was drawing, we discussed them to ensure a mutual understanding. There were some terms that Andrew didn't understand, so they were removed or renamed. He also identified two more feelings which were significant to him – 'embarrassed' and 'nervous' – so we included them in the drawings (Figure 9.1).

*Figure 9.1 Andrew's pictures describing emotions*

I asked Andrew if he would use his own pictures to answer my questions. What follows is a transcript of the interview that I recorded.

*Me:* Which picture *best* describes how you feel when you go into the college building at the start of the day?

*Andrew:* Calm. [*Pointing to the picture.*]

*Me:* Are there any other pictures which *also* describe how you feel when you go into the college building at the start of the day?

*Andrew:* Confident. Confident that I will do well... A bit nervous.

*Me:* OK. Which picture *best* describes how you feel when you're waiting in the foyer?

*Andrew:* [*Hesitation*]... Bored.

*Me:* Are there any other pictures which *also* describe how you feel when you're waiting in the foyer?

*Andrew:* Tired...more than tired...sleepy.

*Me:* Which picture *best* describes how you feel when you're working in Loxshop?

*Andrew:* Calm.

*Me:* Is it calm or is it something else?

*Andrew:* Calm.

*Me:* Are there any other pictures which *also* describe how you feel when you're working in Loxshop?

*Andrew:* Bored...tired...happy.

*Me:* Which picture *best* describes how you feel when you're in ...'s lessons?

*Andrew:* [*Immediately*] Calm. And confident. I don't get excited and I feel I can do well.

*Me:* Are there any other pictures which *also* describe how you feel when you're in ...'s lessons?

*Andrew:* No. Just calm and confident.

*Me:*    Which picture *best* describes how you feel when you're in …'s lessons?

*Andrew:*    Exactly the same!

*Me:*    Remind me which picture that was.

*Andrew:*    [*Pointing to the pictures*] Calm and confident.

*Me:*    That's great.

*Me:*    Which picture *best* describes how you feel when you're in a maths lesson?

*Andrew:*    [*Thinks*]… A bit worried…confused?

*Me:*    Are there any other pictures?

*Andrew:*    No. Just worried and confused.

*Me:*    OK. Now, which picture *best* describes how you feel when you're in your English lessons.

*Andrew:*    [*Immediately*) Happy and relaxed.

*Me:*    Are there any other pictures which *also* describe how you feel when you're in your English lessons?

*Andrew:*    No. Happy and relaxed [*impatiently*].

*Me:*    Which picture *best* describes how you feel when you're on your own at *break* times?

*Andrew:*    [*Thinks*] …a bit bored…calm.

*Me:*    Are there any other pictures which *also* describe how you feel when you're on your own at *break* time?

*Andrew:*    No. Bored and calm.

*Me:*    Which picture *best* describes how you feel when you're on your own at lunch times?

*Andrew:*    [*Immediately*] The same.

*Me:*    Are there…?

*Andrew:*    [*Interrupting*] Nooooooo [*smiling*].

*Me:*    Which picture *best* describes how you feel when you're in the dining room having your lunch?

*Andrew:*    [*Immediately*] Happy.

*Me:*    Are there any other pictures?

*Andrew:*    No [*insistently*].

*Me:*          That's great. You've done really well. Thanks very
               much.

Andrew was ready for a break at this point.

*Me:*          Would you like to have a break for five minutes?

*Andrew:*      Hmm… I think I'll do some more drawing.

Not everything fitted with my perception of things and there
were a few discrepancies in Andrew's answers, so I decided to ask
the following supplementary questions. This time I used the
pictures to identify the feelings that I was questioning Andrew
about.

*Me:*          [*Pointing to the picture*] Are there ever any times at
               college when you feel frightened?

*Andrew:*      I don't think so. No.

*Me:*          Are there times when you feel worried?

*Andrew:*      If I think I've done something wrong.

*Me:*          Is it easy to know if you've done something wrong, or
               is it difficult?

*Andrew:*      [*Unable to answer because I had confused him by asking two
               things.*]

*Me:*          Is it difficult to know when you've done something
               wrong?

*Me:*          [*Repeats again*]

*Andrew:*      No. Not really.

*Me:*          OK.

*Me:*          Do you ever feel confused when you're at college?

*Andrew:*      Sometimes.

*Me:*          When?

*Andrew:*      If I don't know where to go, or when timetables are
               changing around.

*Me:*          Was that at the beginning of the year, or is it still
               confusing now? [*another confusing question*]

*Andrew:*     I'm not confused at the moment. It was mainly at the beginning of the year.

*Me:*     Do you ever feel embarrassed when you're at college?

*Andrew:*     No.

*Me:*     What about…?

*Andrew:*     [*Interrupts*] Only that time.

*Me:*     OK. We won't talk about that if you don't want to.

*Me:*     Do you ever feel unintelligent? [*This was a specific term that Andrew had identified and added.*]

*Andrew:*     No…Well…yes and no.

*Me:*     Explain to me what you mean.

*Andrew:*     [*Unable to answer.*]

*Me:*     What about in lessons?

*Andrew:*     What if I get the answers wrong?

*Me:*     Does that make you feel unintelligent?

*Andrew:*     [*Hesitation*]…Yes.

*Me:*     Mmm.

*Me:*     Do you ever feel nervous when you're at college?

*Andrew:*     Only when I first got there.

*Me:*     How long did that feeling last for?

*Andrew:*     [*Thinks*] … Until I saw you waiting in the foyer.

*Me:*     Uh huh.

*Me:*     What about feeling lonely?

*Andrew:*     Definite 0 per cent!… Nil point!

*Me:*     There are times at college when you are on your own?

*Andrew:*     But I don't feel lonely.

*Me:*     How do you feel?

*Andrew:*     A bit bored.

*Me:*     Is that all?

*Andrew:*     And calm.

*Me:*     Do you feel bored a lot or a little?

*Andrew:*     Bit of both actually.

| | |
|---|---|
| *Me:* | Do you know why you feel bored? |
| *Andrew:* | [*Abruptly*] There's nothing to do! |
| *Me:* | Are there times when you feel tired? |
| *Andrew:* | Yes – when I've had a hard day…when I've been in Loxshop…when I get home from college. |
| *Me:* | Are there lots of times when you're tired? |
| *Andrew:* | Actually yes! |
| *Me:* | OK. |
| *Me:* | Tell me, how did you feel when you first went to college? |
| *Andrew:* | Confident…When I first went to college I was confident and nervous at the same time. |
| *Me:* | What about now? [*a bit ambiguous*] |
| *Andrew:* | Well I… [*pause*] |
| *Me:* | How do you feel now? Are you still confident? |
| *Andrew:* | [*Immediately*) Yes. |
| *Me:* | Are you ever naughty at college? |
| *Andrew:* | Absolutely no! |
| *Me:* | Do you ever feel excited when you're at college? |
| *Andrew:* | I'm excited about France… And the barge trip. |
| *Me:* | What about feeling giddy? [*This is a Sheffield term which means over-excited or silly.*] |
| *Andrew:* | Giddy? Not that I know of. |
| *Me:* | What about the times in Loxshop? [*referring to an incident*] Was that giddy? |
| *Andrew:* | No. |
| *Me:* | Explain to me what that was. |
| *Andrew:* | [*Pause*] |
| *Me:* | If it wasn't giddy, what was it? |
| *Andrew:* | Happy. |
| *Me:* | Oh. |
| *Me:* | When do you feel happy? |
| *Andrew:* | Most of the time. |

*Me:*     How much of the time is that?

*Andrew:*   Sometimes.

*Me:*     Is that a lot or a little?

*Andrew:*   A little.

*Me:*     You've already told me that you feel calm at college.

*Andrew:*   Yeah!

*Me:*     When do you feel most calm and relaxed?

*Andrew:*   Mmm [*thinks*]. At break times.

*Me:*     Are there any other times?

*Andrew:*   At home.

*Me:*     What about other times when you're at college?

*Andrew:*   In the Loxshop when there's nothing to do.

*Me:*     Aren't you bored then?

*Andrew:*   Sometimes.

*Me:*     What's the difference between being relaxed and bored?

*Andrew:*   [*Quickly*] Dunno.

*Me:*     OK.

*Me:*     Do you like college, Andrew?

*Andrew:*   You bet!

*Me:*     Which do you like best? College or school?

*Andrew:*   Definitely college!

*Me:*     I think we'll stop there, Andrew. You've done really well and been ever so helpful. Thank you.

*Andrew:*   You're welcome.

I had felt concerned before about Andrew's aloneness. He was (and still is) a very well-liked member of his peer group, but he was often seen around college at lunchtimes on his own. This had worried me, as I would have felt very lonely in this situation. Andrew's emphatic answers really caused me to rethink and re-evaluate my perceptions. He was never lonely. This was an emotion which I had attributed incorrectly to him.

Andrew's second year has been even more successful than the first. With the exception of his English lesson, he is fully independent. One of the biggest factors which has made this possible is the development of a close working relationship between the autism-specific support staff and the Retail staff. Close professional relationships and good communication have meant that, even though Andrew is now almost fully independent, he is still supported, but from a distance. This has enabled him to develop socially and even to make friends, which at one time would have been thought extremely unlikely. Andrew has even managed to attend the residential component of the course without specialist support.

Andrew was able to go on a trip to France with his friends from college. More importantly, he was able to help finance this trip with the money he earned at Sainsbury's. Sometimes I go to the store to shop when Andrew is working. His confidence has grown and he knows the jobs he has to do. He is part of the team. I enjoy standing and watching as he chats to customers. I overheard one customer ask Andrew about the availability of some food item. Much to my delight, he said that he had not heard of this item but he would go and find somebody who might be able to assist. He returned very quickly with a colleague who pointed this customer in the right direction.

Recently, I had one of those mid-aisle trolley collisions. To my horror, I knocked over a large display of electric lightbulbs. Within ten seconds of my embarrassing mistake, a quiet and calm voice behind me said, 'Can I help you with that, Sir?' As I turned to see Andrew, what I wanted to do was burst with pride and tell every other shopper that this was someone with a severe communication disorder who had seen what had happened and had come to my rescue. In reality no one noticed and I just blurted out my apologies and while thanking Andrew, moved quickly away from the scene of destruction. This was one foolish customer and a member of staff from Sainsbury's doing his job, just the way it should be. He got back at me later when packing my bag. Andrew commented, in rather too loud a voice for my liking, 'It was really funny when you knocked that stuff over.' And I suppose it was.

We were keen to learn how Andrew's mother viewed the last seven years, and so the following opinions are all her own:

> Andrew had been attending The Rowan School at primary level, and although he had made excellent progress, it became clear that there was no suitable secondary provision for children with his specific needs.
>
> I had mixed feelings when Andrew started at The Resource. Andrew and Shaun were undoubtedly guinea pigs, but I was sure they would not be allowed to fail. I was anxious about how Andrew would cope with being in a large hostile environment, where not many people knew about Andrew's special needs and how to access his potential. I was also worried about bullying and although this reared its ugly head a couple of times, it did not cause huge problems.
>
> While some mainstream teachers were very receptive to the needs of Andrew in a whole class environment, others were distinctly hostile, so his timetable was carefully tailored to his needs and staff enthusiasm.
>
> Communication was maintained by use of the dictaphone. It certainly made the exchange of information a great deal easier than the home/school book of old.
>
> The staff did some excellent work with Andrew's fellow classmates, explaining about autistic spectrum disorders and that the things that they take for granted could be what Andrew found most difficult.
>
> Andrew took to what I thought would be difficult areas like a duck to water. History was taught in such a stimulating way that Andrew really loved it, as he did Design and Technology and Art where he produced some fabulous material. French was challenging, but in an odd sort of way, it actually helped Andrew learn about the 'bare bones' of how people communicate, which increased his

understanding of some of the syntax in English as well as French.

We slowly introduced Andrew to travelling independently on the bus. Most bus drivers were very understanding of Andrew, but on a couple of occasions, the driver's unwillingness to be flexible or sympathetic led to huge problems. There was an incident of bullying that occurred on the bus over a number of weeks. This was reported to staff in The Resource. Staff identified who was responsible and explained about Andrew's needs. The alleged bullies were told that Andrew had been made to feel intimidated by some anonymous boys. In effect, staff asked the bullies to report on their bullying. By doing so, the bullies gained an insight into autism and the bullying did stop.

Andrew used The Resource as a safe haven and retreated there quite a lot, especially at lunchtimes. He made mainstream friends who enjoyed his company. Andrew ran the lunchtime sale of ice creams and lollies.

The germ of an idea about work experience to help Andrew's life skills and to keep him focused on tasks came about in his third year at King Ecgbert's, and gripped his enthusiasm in a big way. He had lots of preliminary visits to ease him into the new environment and his first job was helping out in the produce department. His piles of bananas were a work of conceptual art. The highlight of his morning was the chip butty (otherwise forbidden fruit at home) he could choose for himself in the canteen. He made good working relationships with other staff members and enjoyed the camaraderie they offered, often wanting to shop there at the weekends and greet his new-found friends as he progressed through the aisles.

He was included in Christmas parties and presents. Sainsbury's were very supportive about introducing Andrew into their workforce and the personnel department has shown great vision in their inclusion of Andrew.

Through the difficulties of maintaining the work placement scheme, Andrew became quite a star and was a bit of
a local hero. So much so that my other children who share
a strong facial likeness with each other were often approached and identified as Andrew's brother or sister.

Quite where the time went through those King
Ecgbert days, I'm not sure, but it was soon time to consider what the next steps were going to be. At post-16,
Andrew and his friend Shaun would be the guinea pigs
again, but with continued close supervision to ensure
their success.

College is very different from school. I have had to
come to terms with the fact that it is now Andrew who is
the 'customer', and not me. He is still succeeding on very
different terms. He has moved from being a less able 'fish'
struggling to survive in a very fast moving and competi-
tive school environment, to being a relatively able 'fish'
who is well able to succeed on his particular course where
several of the students have special needs. He still does not
readily make friends and is a bit of a loner, but he does not
appear to miss the socialisation and is content with his
own company.

One big change that Andrew has enjoyed was becoming a paid employee at Sainsbury's. He is paid just above
the minimum wage for his age, but for him it is riches beyond his wildest dreams. A week after payday, he is almost
always broke, so budgeting is a life skill we continue to
focus on. He has a smart new uniform, which he has learnt
to iron for himself. He is still mainly a bag packer, but is
now being used as a 'gofer', replacing items which have
been discarded by customers, so he is getting used to finding his way around the aisles. However, even he gets frustrated when they rearrange the aisles from time to time.

The next hurdle is the move into an appropriate residential setting, as I am sure that with an adequate amount
of support, he could live independently. He says he wants

to live with me for ever, but we both know that this would not be good for either of us. One technical problem in this area is our lack of a social worker. As yet, we do not feature in the social services landscape. Andrew has improved considerably, but when you have known him as long as the 'team' has, his needs are still important to recognise. In many ways, we are a victim of our own success, as we have coped without needing to access welfare support.

Most of the time Andrew is fine and we have become accustomed to his obstinacy, foibles and his rigidities to the point where we have modified our lives and expectations so that they have less impact than they otherwise might have. However sometimes, when we have been lulled into a false sense of security, something happens which pitches us full tilt back into realising that Andrew's autistic behaviour and features have not gone away. They are still lurking and emerge to challenge us when we least expect it. It can be the slightest of triggers, a lost Lego piece, or running out of printer ink. These are things which we find mildly irritating, but which turn Andrew from the loveable big huggy bear that potters amiably through our house into a thundering monster, full of anger and foul language.

Andrew's difficulties have put quite a strain on the family. My marriage ended as my husband and I grew apart. Our daughter has moved to university in Bristol. Although she misses the hustle and bustle of family life (and Mum's cooking/cleaning, etc.) she admits that not having to arbitrate between sibling rows when I was not there has been quite a plus.

The distance we have travelled since Andrew was born 19 years ago in both time and toil has been considerable. It's been a bumpy ride some of the time, but with moments of great joy. Andrew, on the cusp of coming of age, is by and large a happy, content and healthy young man. Most of the time you would barely know of his difficulties. He can communicate effectively, probably as well as many of his peers, and can hold his own in most social settings.

Andrew still comes into The Resource when he is not at college or work. The reception he receives from other pupils in The Resource is tremendous. I feel sure that he is seen as an inspiration for most of the pupils, whether they are academically able or not. He has shown us, them, himself and his employer that with the right support, environment and determination anything is possible.

Andrew still has a long way to go and, like anyone else, his needs will change as he develops and grows. One thing he would love to do is work on the tills at Sainsbury's. We would like this as well because it would make Andrew increasingly attractive as an employee. Sainsbury's argue that Andrew would take longer to train on a till than a 'regular' person. They are probably right. However, once trained (and who should care if this takes three days or three weeks) Andrew will be one of the most efficient, polite and reliable till operators Sainsbury's has ever had. He would become a good trainer of till operators himself. We know this and I am sure you do as well. It will just take a little longer for Sainsbury's to realise and appreciate Andrew's growth and potential. Our role over the next few months and years will be to help Sainsbury's by providing support and encouragement. When they offer Andrew his chance, we will be there alongside him making sure he grabs it tightly with both hands.

# 10

# The Final Chapter?

Our pupils each have a pocket-sized dictaphone. Staff use them to record daily progress, homework and give reminders to parents about the following day's activities. Parents send them back the next day with messages if they wish. Communication is instant and clear. Our second group of Y11 pupils finished their pre-16 education recently. A message was received via the dictaphone on the final day from the mother of Sean, one of these Y11 pupils:

> We'd like to say a very big thank you to all of you that have been involved in Sean's education. It is hard to believe how much progress he has made in the five years he has spent at The Resource. Some of that progress is down to Sean. But, an awful lot is down to the support, help and encouragement he has received. His self-confidence, interpersonal skills and sociability have improved beyond recognition in the last five years. You should all feel extremely proud of the product you have produced in the end, which is Sean.

This is not the final chapter for Sean or Andrew or the students we now support in our post-16 provision. There are many more chapters to come, but only if the right structure, support and guidance are in place. We have made a start with the post-16 provision linked to Sheffield College. The employment support worker our charity appointed three years ago is another bit of the jigsaw in place. However, as has been stressed throughout this book, we do not have all the answers. There are still many bridges for us to cross. The hope always has to be that there will be someone on the other side to meet our young friends and us. We have certainly met some wonderful people on the journey so far.

Shaun, who is now in his second year at college, recently had a four-week work placement in the Sheffield law courts. Shaun visited the courts with a member of staff. The people who work in the courts were superb in their management of the placement. Several of them came to college to meet Shaun and the staff who would be supporting him on the placement. They had a detailed work schedule to give Shaun with what he would be doing on each day. It also included clear information about what he was to wear, what time he was to arrive and who to report to on his arrival. Whenever people put time, effort and thought into the service they offer our students, it is very much appreciated. However, there are many sectors of the community that we need to convince about the superb strengths which people with ASD possess.

The Integration into Work scheme needs to be extended. A greater variety of employers need to be sought so that we can tailor placements to suit the needs of individual pupils. We need a second employment support worker. With no regular source of income to enable trustees to feel secure as employers, this will be difficult, but not impossible. Raising finance to continue projects like Integration into Work is time-consuming and physically draining. Our search for a 'sponsor' to make The Resource financially secure for several years is ongoing.

An employment support worker guiding one young person or adult at a time is not what the politicians would call an efficient use of resources. Learning from our colleagues in the USA, it would be more appropriate to have an employment support worker based in larger centres of employment. Here, one employment support worker could give assistance to an increasing number of young adults and employers. All this would need is office space in appropriate centres of employment. Training would also be required. With a number of our students gaining experience and qualifications in the retail sector, the modern large shopping centre is one obvious example of such a centre of employment. However, there would be a wider variety of jobs than just working in shops. Behind every glossy retail outlet, there will be office-based jobs, catering positions, computer technicians and an army of cleaners. Some retail outlets have multiscreen cinemas, which would provide yet more employment prospects. City centres, with their offices, administrative centres and shops, would be another good employment area in which to put one support worker. Local councils, despite having to manage on decreasing budgets, still offer a range of employment prospects.

We have made several representations to the National Autistic Society to discuss proposals for working together, especially in the areas of employment and post-16 education. The society has a wealth of knowledge and experience. However, their knowledge and experience of students with ASD within mainstream education is limited. As they are a national society we believed, perhaps naively, that we could add to their strengths and experience. We certainly could have benefited from their support and guidance. Access to some of the society's training courses at a cost our limited budget could manage would have been beneficial for staff in The Resource. Sadly, despite our continued efforts, no partnership has been able to develop. It is one of our greatest regrets that The Resource cannot work alongside the National Autistic Society. Greater inclusion and access to education, employment and leisure activities for children and adults with ASD can only be achieved by working together and sharing what limited knowledge and experience we have.

The support and guidance that our ex-pupils will need as they progress through adulthood will be different for each person. What remains true is that all of them will require some level of support. In employment terms, this might range from a monthly phone call to the employer to ensure everything is progressing well, to a high level of support for the first year in a job. People change jobs, or might wish to engage in some retraining. This will need to be facilitated. We cannot talk in terms of an exit strategy. The Resource and its growing team of education, college and charity staff are here for good. We do not see any exit from the lives of Andrew, Shaun or any of the adults who start their secondary education in The Resource at King Ecgbert School. The appropriate structure and support will need to be available for life. One pupil in The Resource became very enquiring about who would be there for him in his old age. His opinion was that he would need support with adult things like cooking and paying the phone bill. However, he was concerned that the difficulties everyone faces in the later stages of their lives may not yet have been considered for people with ASD.

This leads us on to one problem area that will need to be tackled at a national level. If it is accepted that the majority of our young adults, given that they secure employment (either full- or part-time), will be in low-paid jobs, something will need to change to enable this employment to be financially worthwhile. The range of benefits rightly available to adults with a disability could be adversely affected by employment in a low-paid job. It could be more beneficial to redirect some of this money from benefits into paying employment support workers so those adults with disabilities could more easily access the employment market. It is greater access to the employment market that remains one of our ultimate goals. For people with ASD, the structure of school has to be replaced with the structure of college. College has to be replaced with the structure of employment (paid or voluntary). If this does not occur, regression in social and communication skills can be rapid for people with ASD. Nobody would work 35 hours a week in a supermarket if they were only going to be £20 better off. That 'nobody' has to include people with ASD. This difficulty with the benefits system is well known. It needs solving at a national level to aid the number of people with disabilities in employment. Recent figures from the National Autistic Society indicate a 98 per cent unemployment rate (NAS 2000). This figure is unacceptable.

Given that the majority of our ex-students gain employment or supported employment, they may not want to live with their parents beyond a certain age. The age of leaving the parental home will differ with each individual and the family circumstances. The need for supported living facilities that are autism-specific is very apparent in Sheffield. Some of the parents of our pupils have been to view the range of residential provisions offered by Sheffield social services. Some of them are excellent but none of them is specific to the very individual needs of adults with ASD. Staff from The Resource and trustees from our charity have spent time looking at autism-specific residential provisions offered by organisations in other parts of the country. We have learnt a lot about what we would like to offer, given the opportunity to move into the residential sector. We have also looked at the growing number of young adults with ASD that Sheffield social services have to fund who access daycare and residential facilities outside the city. The cost of this to Sheffield social services must be astronomical. Given some initial assistance, we thought that we should be able to offer a residential service in Sheffield for adults with ASD. It is a massive piece in the jigsaw both for the young adults themselves and for their families. This initial assistance is unlikely to come from social services. This is not a criticism of social services. Rather that, like with their colleagues within the education department, there is little planning or finance for achieving long-term goals. Making cuts in the short run satisfies the need to trim annual budgets. Attempting short-term investment in services to make long-term savings is almost impossible to achieve.

The Resource would like to be in a position to offer top quality independent, semi-independent and fully supported living facilities (houses to most people) by the year 2002. We have made a start, as always, by asking the parents of our pupils what they would like for their sons/daughters. This questionnaire is shown in Figure 10.1.

---

## Questionnaire on adult autistic residential/community provision

1. Name of child.
2. Current age.
3. Male/female.
4. Do you envisage your son/daughter living with you in the long term?

   Yes/No
5. If not, at what age would you see your child moving into a suitable supported living environment?
6. Are you aware of any suitable provision currently available in Sheffield? If so, where?
7. If you do wish to have specifically designed residential provisions with skilled staff, what is the nature of the provision that you and your child would wish to have?

   (a) A house with 3–4 other young adults with full-time staff.

   (b) A larger house with 5–10 adults with an appropriate staffing level.

   (c) A larger house with 10–20 adults with an appropriate staffing level.

   (d) A house/flat by him or herself with daily visits from staff and possible access to social events with other young autistic adults.
8. If you envisage your child living with you on a long-term basis, what type of support would you and your child wish to have?

   (a) Support to enable employment to be effective.

---

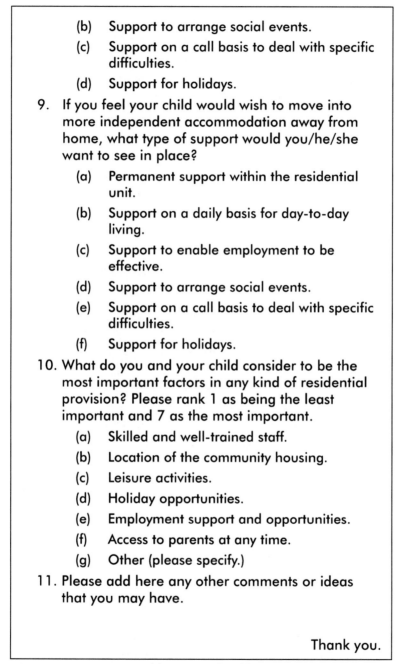

(b)   Support to arrange social events.

(c)   Support on a call basis to deal with specific difficulties.

(d)   Support for holidays.

9.   If you feel your child would wish to move into more independent accommodation away from home, what type of support would you/he/she want to see in place?

(a)   Permanent support within the residential unit.

(b)   Support on a daily basis for day-to-day living.

(c)   Support to enable employment to be effective.

(d)   Support to arrange social events.

(e)   Support on a call basis to deal with specific difficulties.

(f)   Support for holidays.

10. What do you and your child consider to be the most important factors in any kind of residential provision? Please rank 1 as being the least important and 7 as the most important.

(a)   Skilled and well-trained staff.

(b)   Location of the community housing.

(c)   Leisure activities.

(d)   Holiday opportunities.

(e)   Employment support and opportunities.

(f)   Access to parents at any time.

(g)   Other (please specify.)

11. Please add here any other comments or ideas that you may have.

Thank you.

*Figure 10.1 Questionnaire on adult autistic residential/community provision*

What was very clear from the results of the questionnaire was that the majority of parents would like their sons/daughters to move into quality residential facilities before the age of 23. Nothing would appear too strange in this. They see trained and experienced staff as the most important factor in the success of these facilities. Parents would like to see organised leisure activities, with opportunities to follow specific interests. Access to parents at any time is another important issue. Opportunities to go on holiday was also a strongly repeated message. These requests are not unreasonable. This is not a group of rebellious parents. They want the very best for their children. They should be able to plan for the time when they are no longer around to provide the primary care role. Given the struggle for adequate educational provision and respite care that some of them have faced, I believe that they deserve the best. They should not have to face a further battle to obtain residential facilities with which they and their sons/daughters are happy. With our Integration into Work scheme and the massive unemployment difficulties which adults with ASD face, it was inevitable that our set of parents placed employment opportunities and support very high on their list of priorities. Several parents could not prioritise the list of factors that would be important in a residential provision. Instead, they scored all of the factors with a seven. As always, the set of parents we work with now have extremely high expectations. They are also prepared to work with us to achieve the best possible services for people with autism.

The difficulty was that we needed lots of money or a financially secure partner. Getting small amounts of money has been tough enough, so a partnership was the only way forward. Staff in The Resource do not have the necessary expertise or experience in the residential sector. We needed to work alongside people who know what they are doing. Our experience of forming partnerships, with the school, employers and Sheffield College, had always been a rewarding and positive way forward. However, sometimes luck plays its own part as well.

We had a lucky break in this area of work several years ago. Luck should have little to do with obtaining good services for people with autism. The chair of trustees and his wife were at a dinner party when they overheard a man talking about his work with adults on the autistic spectrum. They quickly looked for the earliest opportunity to introduce themselves to this man and to talk to him about the work of The Resource. It transpired that he was the service manager for autism within a charity called the Disabilities Trust. The trust began over 25 years ago by providing residential provisions for people with physical disabilities. They also provide residential options for people with acquired brain injuries. Then, about 12 years ago, the trust began to develop its services for people with autism.

The literature from the Disabilities Trust included phrases such as 'provision based on the needs of the individual' and 'high standards of quality to provide a positive living environment'. The Disabilities Trust appeared to be just what we were looking for in terms of a partner. We were now also confident enough to feel that The Resource had something to offer them, especially in terms of supported employment.

We invited their service manager, Steve Clothier, to come and meet staff and pupils in The Resource. I think there is a danger for people employed in the field of autism that if they enjoy the work, it can take over their lives a little. Steve almost introduced himself as an 'autism anorak'. I had never heard this term but immediately knew what he meant. For every success story we had, he had one to match. We were keen to turn discussion into action, but Steve insisted some of the trustees and staff went to see some of the homes they run in Bedford. This happened quickly and we approved wholeheartedly of what we saw. Here was an organisation that started from the adult and tried to work out what was needed. These individual needs were then met. They had no set models of provision. Services were geared to the needs of individual adults. The trust insisted on working in partnership with a local-based charity. The Disabilities Trust was impressed by our work in the area of employment. The time scale of setting up a residential unit (home) could be as quick as six months, which was too soon for our needs but incredibly exciting.

The next step was to invite Steve to talk to a meeting of all our parents. This was another of those wonderful evenings, not just because of the hope it inspired, but because people had a chance to talk with each other. Parents of children with ASD have become accustomed to fighting for appropriate services, and sometimes for any service at all. At this meeting, parents were faced with a man who was telling them to dream big. It was a new concept for all of us and a difficult adjustment for some of our parents and staff to make so quickly. Parents (and staff) attempted to find the catch in what Steve was saying, only to find that one did not appear to exist. What I liked in particular was that Steve impressed on parents the possibilities of what could be established. These possibilities would be fuelled by a group of young adults who had received a good service so far and would continue to progress socially, academically and vocationally given the right individual structure and services in the future. He stressed that these young people with ASD could become the advocates and trailblazers for future generations. You cannot argue with that kind of vision. What you are faced with, as always, is the work involved in making words turn into reality.

It then went horribly quiet for six months. It is always difficult to cope when nothing appears to be happening. Do you wait, or telephone to stress the urgency of the situation? We decided to wait. Then in October 2000 Steve made arrangements to come and see me. The news was that the Disabilities Trust, in partnership with our charity, wanted to establish a residential service for people with ASD in Sheffield. Those are the kind of days when it is almost impossible to wipe the smile off my face. They make up for the tearful days of the past. Steve met with the trustees two months later to finalise the partnership. With the trust, we will open our first house in 2002. It will be for three or four adults and should be the first of several houses we plan to establish over the next five years. Staff and parents in Sheffield do most of the planning and work, but with the guidance, expertise and finance coming from the Disabilities Trust. We even choose the house, although the trust does have the right of veto. What seemed massive hurdles to staff and trustees appeared to pose the Disabilities Trust little concern. From a partnership point of view, the Disabilities Trust is a dream come true.

This move into the residential sector takes us even further away from the traditional model and idea of education. Perhaps we have had too narrow a focus and a lack of co-ordinated planning and delivery of services across the board for too long. Professionals in education should have an interest in developing adult services. Education and adult services should work with employers if appropriate employment is part of what that individual needs. All professionals should be engaged in the process of establishing or improving residential services for people with ASD. So, instead of this being a massive risk, what we have found is that we have met more people who want to support us and the young adults. The management within Sheffield College is excited by the idea of having residential units in which they can organise and offer courses in independent living. The Disabilities Trust does not currently have a structure in place to offer supported employment. This part of our work appeals to them. Having something to offer in a partnership is imperative and all our hard work over the previous seven years is beginning to reap rewards for some people with ASD in Sheffield.

The time and effort involved in this move into the residential sector brings further excitement to our work, and additional pressures. Fortunately, Sheffield LEA has been cooperative in allowing me time to carry out this work. This cooperation is much appreciated after the battles of the previous seven years. It is refreshing not to have to hear the phrase 'well that's never been done' or 'that's not part of your job description'. All staff in The Resource appreciate being allowed space and time by officers within the education department to carry out this work. Nobody likes or enjoys having to battle with authority.

As this book was nearing completion, we had another break-through that has taken time and effort to achieve. Earlier in this chapter, the need for a sponsor was mentioned. A suitable sponsor has now been found. That sponsor is a charity already heavily involved in the field of autism and research. The Resource had not developed sufficiently over the first six years to make it attractive enough for financial sponsorship. We did not have enough to offer and the staffing base was not secure because of the continuing discussions with Sheffield education authority. The charity was also in its infancy. Our new sponsorship (for the next three years) has been offered on the condition that The Resource and its work can have a national impact. The authors would not be so presumptuous as to assume that what our team does can have a national impact. However, what little we have achieved in Sheffield through inclusion and access can be dupli-cated elsewhere if the human desire and will is there. As we see more integrated resources for pupils with ASD established in other areas of the country, my hope is that they do not have to go through the same trials and tribulations that we did.

Some of this sponsorship money has been used to promote three of the six support workers internally. They will have extra responsibilities out of school hours and will also be instrumental in setting up conferences and workshops in Sheffield in order to let parents and professionals learn more about our work. These same parents and professionals will bring their experiences and knowledge about autism with them, and so we will learn a little more. This sharing of experience and working practices is so important if we are all to work more effectively for the benefit of children, teenagers and adults with ASD. The three support workers deserve this extra salary, as do all six at The Resource. Charities should not have to supplement salaries which are inade-quate, but that's the way it is. From my point of view, I have retained the services of three excellent members of the team.

They have gained new confidence from the extra responsibility they have taken on. They make my working life a little easier.

This is a long way on the journey from the two pupils we started with in The Resource in 1994. One the other hand, maybe it is not very far at all. We could have moved faster and further with better financial investment and fewer hurdles put in our path. Working in any part of the public sector in Britain generally means never having it easy.

Seven years into our journey is not the right time to reflect on what has been achieved. There is little time for reflection and far more important things to do. Progress and a small degree of achievement have their own way of encouraging staff to push back the next boundary, knock on the next door or rise to the next challenge. Pupils continue to achieve success in a variety of ways. With high expectations of both pupils and staff, the right conditions for future success are perhaps now in place. Parents become less protective and more optimistic as they see their son/daughter achieve in and out of school. Staff become more confident in their own abilities and increasingly courageous in what is attempted with individual pupils. Students come back to The Resource from college and inspire the next generation of youngsters. New pupils continue to teach staff about autism and serve as a continual reminder that no one's learning curve is ever complete. People in school, college and places of employment continue to learn about the disability of autism, and some are big enough to concede that their ideas and conceptions have been forced to change because of our students.

There are no short cuts that we can take to speed up this progress, nor can we turn round to people and say 'I told you so'. We can only continue to provide and improve the necessary support and guidance that we hope enables and empowers young people with ASD to flourish. The process will never be complete, but it is hoped that it will become a little easier if the profile of people with autism is continually raised. Every parent and profes-sional has a role to play in this process. Many people with ASD have the most important role to play, if we can provide the services and support they require. Good quality inclusion and integration is one way to raise the profile of children and teenagers with ASD.

At some point in the near future, pressure will need to be applied to national politicians to gain their support both morally but, perhaps more importantly, financially. National funding for employment support workers must be more forthcoming if the disgraceful unemployment rate among people with ASD is to be substantially reduced. The foundations for this reduction in unemployment must begin at school. People who work with teenagers with ASD in schools must receive encouragement to make employment placements part of their curriculum. Teachers should not have to be brave or step outside the law in order to benefit the pupils they are working with. Legislation in relation to employment of people with any kind of disability must be given more 'teeth'.

The pressures will always be there. I am sure that every professional in the field sometimes experiences the feeling that one day things will go wrong and one will be caught out as being a fraud. In 20 years' time, professionals and parents may look back on our efforts with laughter and incredulity. However, accepting that we continue to make mistakes in this imperfect world, I hope they look back and at least acknowledge the effort.

One boy in The Resource saw the stack of paper involved in writing this book and asked what it was all about. I told him that the book was about The Resource, that it was about all of us. He smiled and said that at least this book would have a happy ending. We are a long way from a happy ending, but with a team of 12 staff all pulling in the same direction, backed by supportive parents and trustees, who knows where the journey will lead us over the next seven years? The only certainty is that there will be further tears and laughter.

I have made it clear to Andrew, Sean and a number of other pupils and students that when they are old and I am older still, they will have to leave their lovely house together one evening, after having had a hard day at work. They must come and push me in my wheelchair down to the pub and I'll buy them a drink from my pension. They can introduce me to their friends and I can waffle on about what they were all like aged 11. They can tell me about their jobs and latest interests. I can recount embarrassing stories from their younger days. They can tell me to sit quietly and threaten not to take me out again. When they ask me why I am smiling, I'll tell them that maybe the last chapter of the book is almost finished.

# Bibliography

Attwood, T. (1998) *Asperger's Syndrome: A guide for Parents and Professionals.* London: Jessica Kingsley Publishers.

Attwood, T. (2000) 'Should children with autistic spectrum disorders be exempted from doing homework?' *The Morning News* 12, 2.

Clements, J. and Zarkowska, E. (2000) *Behavioural Concerns and Autistic Spectrum Disorders: Explanations and Strategies for Change.* London: Jessica Kingsley Publishers.

Gerland, G. (2000) *Finding Out about Asperger's Syndrome, High Functioning Autism and PDD.* London: Jessica Kingsley Publishers.

Grandin, T. and Scarieno, M. (1986) *Emergence Labelled Autistic.* New York: Warner.

Hipgrave, T. and Newson, E. (1982) *Getting Through to Your Handicapped Child.* Cambridge: Cambridge University Press.

Howlin, P. (1997) *Autism: Preparing for Adulthood.* London: Routledge.

Morgan, H. (1996) *Adults with Autism: A Guide to Theory and Practice.* Cambridge: Cambridge University Press.

National Autistic Society (2000) *Inclusion and Autism – Is It Working?* London: National Autistic Society.

Sacks, O. (1995) *An Anthropologist on Mars.* London: Picador.

Scott-Parker, S. and Zadek, S. (2000) *Unlocking Potential.* London: Employers Forum on Disability.

Segar, M. (1997) *Coping – A Survival Guide for People with Asperger's Syndrome.* London: Kith and Kids.

Tantum, D. (1999) *A Mind of One's Own.* London: National Autistic Society.

Williams, D. (1996) *Autism: An Inside-Out Approach.*

Lightning Source UK Ltd.
Milton Keynes UK
05 December 2009

147082UK00002BA/5/A